The Lucent Library of Historical Eras

Elizabethan England

A History of the Elizabethan Theater

Other titles in the Lucent Library of Historical Eras, Elizabethan England, include:

The Lucent Library of Historical Eras

Elizabethan England

A History of the Elizabethan Theater

Adam Woog

LUCENT BOOKS®

THOMSON

GALE

San Diego • Detroit • New York • San Francisco • Cleveland • New Haven, Conn. • Waterville, Maine • London • Munich

THOMSON
———✦———
GALE

Queen Elizabeth I (seated, top center) enjoys an evening of theater at The Globe.

LIBRARY OF CONGRESS CATALOGING-IN-PUBLICATION DATA

Woog, Adam, 1953–
    A history of the Elizabethan theater / by Adam Woog.
        p. cm. — (Lucent library of historical eras: Elizabethan England)
Includes bibliographical references and index.
Summary: Discusses the development of the English theater during the Elizabethan era,
including the origins of Elizabethan theater and drama, the influence of the queen and
the church, and the impact of various playwrights and actors.
    ISBN 1-59018-099-2 (alk. paper)
    1. Theater—England—History—16th century. 2. English drama—Early modern and
Elizabethan, 1500–1600—History and criticism. I. Title. II. Series.
PN2589 .W66 2003
792'.0942'09031—dc21

                                                                                2001008205

Printed in the United States of America

Contents

Foreword

Looking back from the vantage point of the present, history can be viewed as a myriad of intertwining roads paved by human events. Some paths stand out—broad highways whose mileposts, even from a distance of centuries, are clear. The events that propelled the rise to power of Germany's Third Reich, its role in World War II, and its eventual demise, for example, are well defined and documented.

Other roads are less distinct, their route sometimes hidden from view. Modern legislatures may have developed from old tribal councils, for example, but the links between them are indistinct in places, open to discussion and interpretation.

The architecture of civilization—law, religion, art, science, and government—as well as the more everyday aspects of our culture—what we eat, what we wear—all developed along the historical roads and byways. In that progression can be traced every facet of modern life.

A broad look back along these roads reveals that many paths—though of vastly different character—seem to converge at a few critical junctions. These intersections are those great historical eras that echo over the long, steady course of human history, extending beyond the past and into the present.

These epic periods of time are the focus of Lucent's Library of Historical Eras. They shine through the mists of history like beacons, illuminated by a burst of creativity that propels events forward—so bright that we, from thousands of years away, can clearly see the chain of events leading to the present.

Each Lucent Library of Historical Eras consists of a set of books that highlight various aspects of these major eras. For example, the Elizabethan England library features volumes on Queen Elizabeth I and her court, Elizabethan theater, the great playwrights, and everyday life in Elizabethan London.

The mini-library approach allows for the division of each era into its most significant and most interesting parts and the exploration of those parts in depth. Also, social and cultural trends as well as illustrative documents and eyewitness accounts can be prominently featured in individual volumes.

Lucent's Library of Historical Eras presents a wealth of information to young readers. The lively narrative, fully documented primary and secondary source quotations, maps, photographs, sidebars, and annotated bibliographies serve as launching points for class discussion and further research.

In studying the great historical eras, students also develop a better understanding of our own times. What we learn from the past and how we apply it in the present may shape the future and may determine whether our era will be a guiding light to those traveling future roads.

Introduction
Queen Elizabeth, the Renaissance, and the Stage

The Elizabethan era, the latter half of the sixteenth century, was one of the most exciting periods in England's long and colorful history. All across Europe a new era was dawning, and England was one of its primary leaders.

England had once been a small island nation torn apart by religious battles, physically isolated from the rest of Europe, and relatively unsophisticated in its customs and outlook. During the Elizabethan era, however, it completed its transformation into a formidable world power.

Much of this change had to do with the country's new monarch. Elizabeth, one of the daughters of King Henry VIII, ascended to the throne in 1558 at the age of twenty-five. As Queen Elizabeth I, she reigned until her death in 1603 when her cousin, James I, succeeded her.

Unlike the symbolic royal family today, a monarch in England during this time was an absolute ruler who wielded great power. Elizabeth's rule was unusually long and eventful, and "Good Queen Bess" was a strong and generally popular monarch.

Good Queen Bess

Elizabeth's reign was a period of unprecedented development, political optimism, economic growth, and social unity. Militarily, the nation was stronger than it had ever

Queen Elizabeth I (1553–1603) transformed England from a tiny nation torn by strife into a politically unified global power.

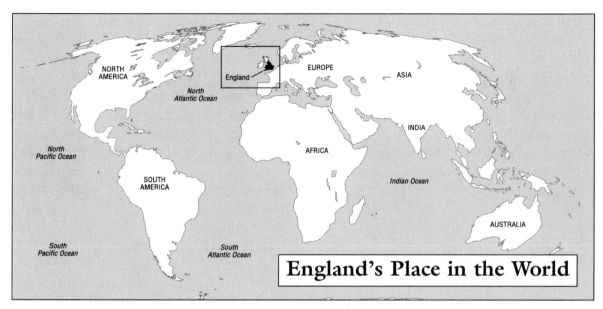

England's Place in the World

been. Socially and politically, its many factions were joined, at least to a degree, into a single cohesive unit.

Elizabeth welcomed changes in her country's long-stagnant religious order. She encouraged scientific discoveries that radically altered the lives of her subjects. She also fostered the exploration of faraway lands, a practice that introduced strange and exotic new goods to her amazed people. Because of all this, England experienced an unprecedented feeling of security, patriotism, and optimism.

The forward-looking attitude of the English people—and their monarch—was not an isolated event. The Renaissance, an extraordinary burst of intellectual learning, discovery, and thinking, was sweeping across Europe.

Enlightenment

"Renaissance" means rebirth. The name refers to the movement, which began in Italy, that swept away the previous historical period, the Middle Ages, also called the Medieval era. In place of the Middle Ages' fear, repression, and ignorance, the Renaissance was a period of exciting new philosophies and the reintroduction of timeless ancient ones.

During the Middle Ages, which lasted nearly a thousand years, the Church dominated virtually all aspects of life. Intellectual, scientific, and artistic exploration were discouraged or banned unless related directly to the teachings of the Church. Heretics—those who dared question the Church's authority—were banished, tortured, or killed.

When this dark period began to lift around the beginning of the sixteenth century, many things occurred. One aspect of the new age was a renewal of interest in the brilliant but long-forgotten literature, art, and philosophy of ancient Greece and Rome.

Europeans were inspired by this ancient wisdom, and they also made dozens of earth-shaking new discoveries and achievements on their own. These included exploring far-off lands, especially the New World of the Western Hemisphere, and adopting new scientific discoveries such as the revolutionary Copernican system of astronomy. They embraced powerful new technologies—the printing press, the compass, and gunpowder. Literacy grew rapidly as printing presses made books affordable and the Church's dominance over education waned. Furthermore, the Renaissance witnessed a decline in the ancient feudal system of agriculture, which had long maintained a deep social divide between the noble and peasant classes.

Hunger for Knowledge

The dominance of the Church during the Middle Ages included an insistence that all art be directly related to religious teachings. As the Church's grip on intellectual life began to weaken, however, artists of all kinds began exploring new territory. One element in the Renaissance's potent mix of ideas was theater. Prior to the Renaissance,

the only dramatic art allowed had been a crude version that taught religious lessons. The Elizabethans changed this forever.

During the Elizabethan era a professional class of actors and writers emerged for the first time in England's history. They were inspired by ancient Greek and Roman theater; they absorbed the Renaissance's explosion of learning and exploration; and they incorporated into their work exciting new developments in stagecraft, acting style, and writing.

The result was a stunning level of sophistication never before seen—and a wealth of plays that mirrored the exciting changes taking place. Elizabethan theater also reflected England's rich history and the experiences—alternately thrilling and terrifying—of daily life in its central city, London.

For modern theater-lovers, Elizabethan theater provides a vivid glimpse of a long-gone way of life. Its plays proved to be so strong, lively, and interesting that they are still admired, studied, and produced today, some four hundred years later.

A Golden Age of Theater

Elizabethan theater, like all good art, reflects the times in which it is created. As the English theater world developed and matured during this period of rapid change and ferment, it mirrored all the qualities, good and bad, of English society.

Because Elizabethan plays often portray contemporary settings and everyday situations, they offer modern viewers a valuable look at what daily life was like for Elizabethans. For instance, Elizabethan theater is often preoccupied with violence and death. This is characteristic of the period. Hardship, death, war, madness, murder, greed, and bloody revenge were common elements in everyday life—and so in drama of the day as well.

At the same time, Elizabethan theater also reflected another characteristic of the Elizabethan age: a sensitivity to beauty and grace. Elizabethans appreciated subtle refinements in poetry, literature, and music. Passionate love, high adventure, romance, and forgiveness are thus common themes. Furthermore, Elizabethans loved to laugh, and so comedy was an ever popular aspect of their drama.

Typical of the Elizabethan age, as in virtually all other eras, was a love of stories. Whether romantic, tragic, uplifting, gory, noble, evil, funny, or some combination thereof, good stories were endlessly fascinating to audiences of the time.

Elizabethans loved elaborate and clever wordplay, and this love is reflected in the theater of the period. Theater historians Thomas Marc Parrott and Robert Hamilton Ball note that this love of language created a highly romantic and lyrical dramatic style: "The Elizabethan age was the most musical in English history, and this music poured into the language of the drama. . . . All the romance of the Elizabethan age, its awareness of new words, its love of adventure, its worship of beauty, find fit expression in the poetry of Elizabethan drama."[1]

More Reflections

Elizabethan culture is characterized, in part, by a deep and widely held belief in the supernatural. Ghosts, witches, magicians, fairies, and other supernatural creatures thus appear frequently throughout Elizabethan drama. Ghosts play important roles, for instance, in such Shakespearean plays as *Hamlet, Julius Caesar,* and *Richard III*. Witches—the "three weird sisters"—are well-known figures in *Macbeth*. A magician, Prospero, is the

The three witches of Shakespeare's Macbeth *sing to a phantom baby in a modern production of the timeless tragedy.*

hero of *The Tempest*. And tiny fairy creatures play a major role in *A Midsummer Night's Dream*.

Many broader cultural and social issues are also addressed in Elizabethan theater. Patriotism was an important aspect of the Elizabethan character, for instance, during most of Elizabeth's reign. This feeling is reflected in the era's many "chronicle" or historical plays, which glory in England's strength.

The issue of censorship was also part of the Elizabethan dramatic world, both directly and indirectly. Playwrights were forbidden to criticize Elizabethan nobility, especially the queen. However, they could satirize or comment on social conditions if they did so in a roundabout way. Ben Jonson's comedies, for example, often make fun of an emerging class of society during his time, the newly rich merchant class.

However, plays of the Elizabethan era are not important simply for the insights they give modern viewers into this period of history. They also are vitally important to the history of drama because of how they advanced the technical aspects of playwriting and acting. Earlier theater in England had been quite crude and simple. By the time the Elizabethan era was over, however, English theater had become sophisticated and complex in such technical aspects as language, plot and character development, and stage presentation.

Many scholars and theater fans argue that the Elizabethan era is crucial to theater history for one reason above all—the existence of William Shakespeare, whom many

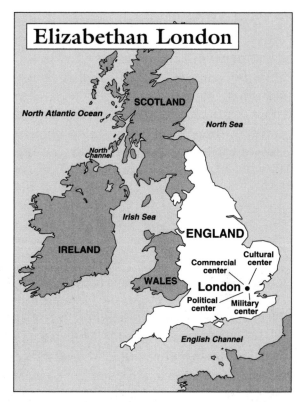

Elizabethan London

consider the greatest dramatist of all time in any language. However, others feel that the Elizabethan period would be considered a vital period even without Shakespeare's brilliant contributions. Theater historian R.C. Bald asserts, "Even if Shakespeare had never lived, the last fifteen years of Queen Elizabeth's reign and the reign of King James I would still be the greatest period in the history of the English drama." [2]

London Central

Elizabethan theater developed and matured in the city of London. Then, as now, it was the vibrant heart of English life. Life there was lived in an atmosphere that was—well, dramatic.

London's population grew steeply during Elizabethan times, from about one hundred thousand in 1550 to about two hundred thousand by 1600. This figure is small compared to the great cities of modern times, but it was large enough by the standards of the day to make London a big city—a lively center of commerce, politics, and art, and a place of nonstop action and bustle.

London was, first of all, England's political center. Parliament and other important government institutions were headquartered there, so important events and pivotal decisions affecting the entire country occurred in the city every day. Furthermore, Elizabeth and her many court members lived in London for much of each year, and their frequent, highly dramatic appearances in public lent color and excitement to life in the city.

London was also a center for commerce both within England and for the world at large. Its dozens of prosperous craft guilds represented various highly skilled trades. Its international trading companies, such as the Muscovy Company and the East India Company, conducted lucrative operations in far-off lands. Its banking institutions were the lifeblood of England's commerce, and its law schools and universities turned out a steady stream of men skilled in conducting such business.

The city was also a hotbed of religious controversy in a nation that was, overall, deeply religious. Earlier in the sixteenth century, Elizabeth's father, Henry VIII, had split from the Roman Catholic Church to form the Church of England, his own version of Protestantism. The conflicts between Catholic and Protestant factions created by this split continued into Elizabethan times. Like her father, Elizabeth was a Protestant, so she was in constant danger from Catholic loyalists who wanted to replace her on the throne.

Furthermore, London was a center for England's mighty military force. A major naval dockyard was located at Deptford on the south bank of the city's River Thames. London also provided a significant proportion of England's troops for service overseas.

Finally, the city was a magnet for the country's artistic life. Artists, musicians, students, and writers naturally gravitated to London, as they do to the great cities of the world today.

The City of London

The heart of this metropolis was a small area known as The City of London. This central borough still bore remains of its original Roman walls. Today this section, called simply The City, remains the financial center of London.

The River Thames was London's lifeline, winding its way through the middle of the city and serving as a "highway" for the countless ships and boats laden with people and goods that constantly sailed into, around, and out of London. According to a contemporary historian, William Camden, the Thames was so crowded with water traffic that it resembled "a very wood of trees disbranched to make glades and let in light, so shaded it is with masts and sails."[3]

The great cathedral of St. Paul's, rising high above the other buildings, was The City of London's single most distinctive visual feature. Westminster Abbey in the neighboring borough of Westminster was also a striking landmark. Extravagant townhouses of the rich with lush gardens leading down to the banks of the Thames were further focal points.

Large and sumptuous buildings such as these contrasted sharply with the twisted, cramped maze of streets and seedy neighborhoods that surrounded them. The condition of its public streets, meanwhile, underscored the fact that London was, in many ways, a dark, dangerous, and dirty place to live.

Smelly Old Town

The differences in the lives of the poor and the rich were starkly outlined in London. Poverty, unemployment, and homelessness were commonplace among the "ordinary" citizens of the city. Even for the well-off, however, daily life was often unpleasant.

For one thing, the city stank. Animals roamed freely in the streets. Neither the rich nor the poor bathed regularly, believing it

Elizabeth's father, King Henry VIII, broke with the Roman Catholic Church to establish the Church of England. Here, the king is presented with the first English translation of the Bible.

Although the streets of London in Elizabethan times bustled with activity, they were gloomy and filthy.

bad for the health, so strong odors were accepted facts of life. Perfume sellers always did a brisk business. Also, there were no sewers in London. Garbage and human waste were simply dumped in the streets or in the river.

These streets were crowded and full of activity, but dark and dismal even in daylight. This was due in part to London's weather, overcast and rainy for much of the year, and in part to the deep shadows cast by precariously built housefronts jostling for space. Most of the homes and shops within these housefronts were overcrowded, and their inner rooms were badly lit and poorly ventilated.

London's crowded, dirty conditions fostered widespread and frequent disease. Not even the wealthy were isolated from this horror. Terrifying outbreaks of plague, cholera, smallpox, and other diseases were commonplace. These epidemics had serious effects on the theater, since the theaters would be closed for long periods of time during outbreaks of disease.

Disease and Crime

Thousands died or were disfigured during these epidemics. Londoners became accustomed to seeing dead bodies lying in the streets or being hauled away to common graves. The cramped dark streets of the city also attracted many criminals—murderers, muggers, shoplifters, and more. Gambling, drinking, and prostitution were widespread and essentially uncontrolled. For those criminals who were caught by authorities, death was a common outcome.

The executions of criminals were frequent and hugely popular public events. As warnings to others, the authorities often allowed hanged criminals to twist in the wind for days, or they displayed severed heads on spikes. Such sights sometimes inspired theatrical presentations of the day to heights of grisly violence. Writer Simon Trussler notes, "This was an age of close proximity to death and decay, in which the goriest of stage spectacles might be outdone on the streets outside by the agonies of a plague victim, or the sight of a traitor's head maggot-ridden on its spike at the foot of London Bridge."[4]

"Lusty at Legs"

Nonetheless for all of its grimness, life in London could be thrilling. Something amazing to see or do lay around every corner, and the streets, constantly buzzing with activity, provided a nonstop show. A playwright of the era, Thomas Dekker, described a typical scene:

> In every street, carts and coaches make such a thundering as if the world ran upon wheels. At every corner, men,

A mass grave is readied outside the city walls for victims of the plague. Deadly epidemics were a common occurrence in sixteenth-century England.

women, and children meet in such shoals that posts are set up . . . to strengthen the houses, lest with jostling one another they should shoulder them down.

Besides, hammers are beating in one place, tubs hooping in another, pots clinking in a third, water tankards running at a tilt in a fourth. Here are porters sweating under burdens, there, merchants' men bearing bags of money. Chapmen (as if they were at leapfrog) skip out of one shop into another. Tradesmen . . . are lusty at legs and never stand still. [5]

Elizabethan playwrights often used such lively street scenes as inspiration for their works. The rowdy town square scene that opens *Romeo and Juliet,* for instance, is set in Verona, Italy, but would not have been out of place in a typical London street.

Development of a Native Theater

The writers and actors of the early Elizabethan theater could draw on many other sources of inspiration. They studied newly rediscovered tragedies and comedies of the ancient Greeks and Romans. They observed religious educational dramas, hallmarks of the Middle Ages, that were still performed in church or by amateur actors honoring their patron saints. They were inspired by itinerant performers such as minstrels, jugglers, and dancers.

These playwrights then merged all these elements into a new form of theater. This native form of theater was unlike anything else seen in England and unlike other forms of drama developing elsewhere in Europe. The maturing Elizabethan drama, by fusing these many elements together, was far stronger and richer than the crude religious theatricals that preceded it and formed its primary roots.

Chapter

2

The Origins of the Elizabethan Theater

The dominance of the Church during the Middle Ages was so strong that it extended even to dramatic performances. Medieval Church leaders vigorously condemned all nonreligious forms of theater, considering them ungodly and wicked. Religious dramas were thus one of the few forms of theater allowed in England during these long centuries.

However, Church leaders also recognized that drama could be used for its own religious and educational purposes. Theater historian J.L. Styan writes, "It is a matter of great importance for the history of the English stage that the Church recognized drama as a force to be harnessed and chose to use it to teach the people about the Scriptures and to glorify God."[6]

Early Religious Plays

Only a few forms of performance were tolerated in England during the Middle Ages. Among these forms were those presented by itinerant performers—wandering entertainers, street jugglers, or musicians who traveled from town to town. While such performers were not strictly illegal, Church officials and many town authorities frowned on them. More to their liking was another type of performance, one that flourished far more readily: dramas performed in churches to illuminate stories from the Bible.

The plots of these plays, which told such familiar tales as the resurrection of Jesus, were simple and direct. Male priests assumed all the roles, with few if any props. The dialogue was simply spoken or sung recitation,

An actor portrays Jesus in a modern production of a medieval passion play. Such dramas were acted out during the Middle Ages to illuminate stories from the Bible.

and there was no major dramatic action. The language was Latin, the language of the Church. Educated people understood it, but few outside the Church understood it well, if at all.

Church leaders realized, however, that they needed more than this simple form of entertainment to hold the attention of audiences accustomed to the crowd-pleasing antics of street performers. The religious dramas therefore slowly changed over time, becoming more easily understandable and attractive to a lay audience—that is, to regular parishioners, not clergymen.

The clergy accomplished this change by incorporating simple but vivid techniques such as decorating a part of the church altar to resemble the tomb from which Jesus arose. Such techniques proved to be effective and popular; in short, they worked. Elizabethan scholar David Klein comments, "A scene like this the people could understand; they liked it, and wanted more of the same kind."[7]

The Mystery Cycles

Over time, more and more of these brief but popular plays were added to the repertoire of the clergy in a given church. Some, called miracle plays, depicted the lives and accomplishments of saints. Others depicted familiar Bible scenes such as Adam and Eve, Abraham and Isaac, Noah and the Flood, and the life of Christ.

These stories from the Bible were eventually grouped together by clergy in various towns to form strings of short plays. These series of plays were called mystery cycles. By the thirteenth and fourteenth centuries, the cycles had evolved into lengthy and elaborate pageants that often took a full day or two to unfold.

It has been estimated that over one hundred towns in the British Isles celebrated festivals at least once a year at which mystery cycles were performed. The texts of only four of these mystery cycles have survived in English, however. (Some villages in southern Germany, western Austria, and Switzerland still perform their versions of mystery plays on a regular basis. They are often called passion plays.)

Despite the lack of evidence about mystery cycles in English, scholars have been able to determine quite a bit of information about them. For one thing, they were extremely popular. In part, this popularity was the result of two important new elements.

One new element was that lay members of the church were taking part in them and in some cases assuming most of the responsibility for mounting them. Also, instead of Latin, a language few parishioners understood, they were by the late Middle Ages performed in everyday English.

These two developments meant that ordinary people, including even uneducated peasants, were now able to appreciate and understand the plays in ways they never could before. Historian J.L. Styan writes, "This was the first time in England that a form of theatre had been created which included a wide range of ranks and classes in medieval society."[8]

The Guilds Take On Performance

The authors of the mystery cycles are unknown. Probably they were members of the Church clergy. However, much of the work needed to create the plays was performed by the members of various guilds.

Predecessors to modern labor unions, guilds were organizations of trade and craft workers. These guilds became so closely associated with the mystery cycles that they may have lent their name to the plays. The word "mystery," some scholars believe, comes from the word "master," the term then used for craftsmen.

Typically, specific guilds would be responsible for certain sections of the cycles. The plays a given guild mounted would be related to its specific craft or trade. The story of Noah building the Ark, for instance, would be presented by shipbuilders. Jonah and the Whale would be performed by fish sellers and fishermen. The Last Supper would be presented by the baker's guild.

The guilds and clergy were not the only participants in staging the mystery cycles, however. There was so much work to do that virtually every part of a given town played a part in mounting a production. Theater historian David Klein points out that producing a theatrical experience was thus no longer strictly for the clergy: "The first important thing to note about the plays thus produced is that they were a communal affair. They were written for the people, because the people demanded them, and were acted by the people."[9]

Heaven and Hell on Stage

One aspect of this community involvement was the appointment of a pageant master from among the prominent members of a community. This man acted as an overseer of all the guilds' contributions and collected the pageant-silver, a tax that covered production costs.

This tax was necessary because mystery plays were becoming ever more elaborate in their production. By the late Middle Ages, the dramas were typically performed on special carts, called pageant wagons. These provided portable stages and dressing rooms, all in one. They were outgrowths of smaller wagons that had for centuries been

A crowd of spectators watches as a mystery play is performed on a pageant wagon. By the late Middle Ages, most dramas were played out on such carts.

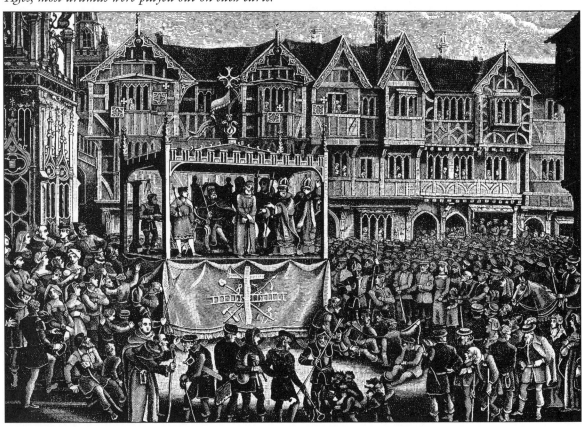

used in Church processions to stage biblical scenes.

Costuming was also becoming increasingly elaborate. Actors playing angels wore wigs made of hemp and donned painted wings and halos. The actor portraying God wore a gilded mask. To achieve the illusion of nudity, Adam and Eve had tight-fitting white leather costumes. Devils wore dark leather suits complete with snouts, claws, and horns.

The use of props and scenery also became more sophisticated. Heaven was typically depicted on the roof of a small pergola at one end of a pageant wagon's stage. Hell was at the other end of the platform— a monstrous head with jaws that opened and closed, allowing smoke and fire and the Devil to appear on cue.

Since the pageant wagons used for mystery cycles were portable, plays did not necessarily have to be performed on church grounds. In fact, as time went on they were more often performed in open public spaces. Theater historian J.L. Styan notes, "The village green and town square provided natural arenas for the unlocalized *platea* [Latin: 'wide street' or open acting space] round which spectators gathered."[10]

The Mystery Cycles Decline

By the early 1500s the Renaissance was beginning to be felt in England, and the mystery cycles began to fall out of favor both with the Church and with audiences. The Church was less interested in supporting them; the plays were increasingly performed away from church grounds, and their value

Mystery plays used sound effects and rich pageantry to dazzle the audience. By the beginning of the sixteenth century, however, the popularity of the genre had begun to wane in England.

as religious education was becoming questionable. Meanwhile, audiences were dissatisfied with the long, rambling texts of the plays. They tended to favor performers such as musicians and jugglers.

The mystery cycles also fell victim to England's increasingly strong religious conflicts. In 1534, Henry VIII broke with the Roman Catholic Church and established the Church of England. The mystery cycles—seen as threats to the ruling Protestant government—officially fell out of royal favor and were suppressed, if not entirely banished. When Henry's daughter Elizabeth became queen in 1558, the suppression of Catholic-related drama continued. The last recorded performances of a mystery cycle were in the 1570s.

Mystery plays are crude, but they were an important early step in the development of British theater and directly influenced the sophisticated plays of the coming Elizabethan era. Historians Thomas Marc Parrott and Robert Hamilton Ball note, "In more ways than one they [mystery plays] laid the foundations of Elizabethan drama; even such masterpieces of that age as [Christopher Marlowe's] *Dr. Faustus* and Shakespeare's Histories show plainly remaining traces of the old Miracle [and mystery] plays."[11]

Morality Plays

Before the Elizabethan theater came into maturity, however, England saw another, transitional type of drama. This style, called the morality play or interlude, combines religious-education drama with more secular (nonreligious) entertainment. The time frame of the morality plays overlapped the later years of the mystery plays and continued after the mystery plays began to be suppressed.

The plots of morality plays are not taken directly from Bible stories, but they are nonetheless often highly religious and moral. They depict the virtues and vices of humankind, pitting good and evil forces against each other to gain control of a man's soul. They thus could mix pious lessons about proper behavior with characters and situations taken from real life, freely combining elements of old-fashioned religious drama with more up-to-date secular ideas.

The English playwrights who created morality plays were not much concerned with the formal rules about theater devised in the Roman and Greek traditions, as were their counterparts elsewhere in Europe. Instead, they used as a base the traditions of their own medieval religious dramas.

They then blended some of the sophisticated theatrical techniques being experimented with in Europe with this "homemade" strain of drama. The result appealed to virtually all segments of society—high- and low-class, rich and poor, piously religious and irreverent.

Making It Exciting

By the early 1500s other changes in drama were taking place in addition to different styles of writing. In particular, the growth of a semiprofessional group of players was underway. These were performers who were not clergymen or even guild members, but simply amateurs from various walks of life. They performed their shows wherever they could, including public squares and the courtyards of inns. These groups were not performing simply for the love of acting or of their religion. They also were in it for the money, and relied for their livelihood on contributions from the crowds that gathered to watch. Thus, to hold the attention of their audiences, they needed to add excitement and entertainment to the moral lessons of their plays.

They accomplished this by adding diversions such as dancing, singing, or juggling to the basic plot. They also added satire to their shows, inventing characters that made fun of such real-life people as physicians, soldiers, judges, and priests. They further added excitement by developing a range of theatrical tricks. For example, a troupe might build anticipation and enthusiasm among their audience by anticipating the arrival of a fearful Devil—but then stop the performance and refuse to introduce this exciting development until enough coins had been thrown their way.

Humanity and Everyman

Because the characters in morality plays portray abstract qualities or ideas, they were given labels rather than real names. Characters often are simply identified by such titles as Charity, Vice, Death, or Youth. Sometimes they have "real" names meant to convey their natures, such as Staunch Goodfellow or Steadfast Faith.

The morality play's typical mixture of religious teaching with everyday life is demonstrated by *The Nature of the Four Elements,* written by John Rastell around 1519. It tells the story of the wicked Sensual Appetite, who leads the pious Humanity astray and tempts him with pleasure. Reality enters the mix when Humanity is taken to a tavern. He has a merry time with characters who have more or less real names: the Taverner, Nell, and Bess. In the end, Humanity sees the error of his ways and returns to the devout life. Before this pious ending arrives, however, both Humanity

and the audience are tempted by the promise of wickedness and entertained by groups of singers and dancers

About sixty morality plays still exist today in English. Probably the best known of these is *Everyman,* which was adapted from a Dutch play, *Elckerlyc. Everyman* is a very short play—only about nine hundred lines—but it is beautiful and simple, solemnly and vividly portraying the themes of death and the fate of the human soul. J.L. Styan comments that these are themes that even modern audiences can relate to: "The coming of death and the moment of dying are subjects of universal and undying appeal, and the play never loses its grip on what is real and human."[12]

Death claims his victim in a scene from a twentieth-century production of the most famous of the existing medieval morality plays, Everyman.

Moving Toward Real Drama

John Heywood's *The Play of the Wether [Weather]* is another example of the early morality play. The dates of its composition and first performance are unknown, although scholars know it was first printed in 1533. The play depicts various people who are brought forth before Jupiter, the king of the gods in ancient Roman mythology. They beg in turn for Jupiter to create weather that would suit them best. Each has conflicting desires, however, so in the end the weather remains unchanged.

Judged by today's standards, plays such as *Everyman, The Nature of the Four Elements,* and *The Play of the Wether* seem little more than slight anecdotes; they hardly could be considered sophisticated drama. Their plots are simple, and their characters are still one-dimensional figures rather than full-blooded people. However, their lengthy dialogues and satirical debates in rhymed dialogue demonstrate the basic elements of what would soon become genuine dramatic form. The morality plays—along with other plays developed during the early 1500s such as the first Histories, lively tales based on real historical incidents—represent another major step toward a maturing English theater.

Classical Models

The next major development required mastering the intricacies of plot and deeper, more varied characterization. To achieve these goals, English playwrights turned to ancient Greek and Roman models for inspiration. After centuries of neglect these complex and highly developed theatrical techniques and philosophies were in favor again.

One of the most important aspects of the Greek and Roman models is the concept of classifying drama as history, tragedy, or comedy. Seneca, a Roman author famed for his tragedies, was especially influential on Renaissance playwrights. They borrowed, for example, Seneca's method of structuring a play into five acts. They also borrowed his use of long recitations in verse with relatively little action on stage.

Seneca was a Roman dramatist whose tragedies heavily influenced Elizabethan playwrights.

One example of an early Elizabethan tragedy along Senecan lines is *Gorboduc,* written by Thomas Sackville and Thomas Norton in 1561. Based on a true incident in British history, it is a serious moral tale warning about the pitfalls of irresponsible government. Typical of straightforward historical drama from this period, meanwhile, is *The Misfortunes of Arthur,* which is about the legendary King Arthur. It was written in 1588 by Thomas Hughes.

Comedy is represented by the anonymous *Gammer Gurton's Needle,* written around 1559. This sophisticated comedy, strongly influenced by Italian theater of the time, concerns the trouble caused by the loss of a highly prized sewing needle.

Getting Real

Probably the best known of the early comedies written in English, however, is Nicholas Udall's *Ralph Roister Doister* (1553). Its title character is a version of the character later perfected as Shakespeare's Falstaff—the boisterous, larger-than-life, braggart soldier.

An audience watching this play quickly learns that Ralph Roister Doister's bark is worse than his bite. One character says that "All the day long is he facing and craking [swaggering and bragging] / Of his great actes in fighting and fraymaking." In reality, however, this blowhard is really only "as fierce as a Cotssold lyon [as brave as a Cotswold sheep]."[13]

Comedies such as this one, along with tragedies and histories, all reflected a new trend in theater of the early Elizabethan period: a growing emphasis on true-to-life situations. There are many ways in which this realism is shown. Tragedies feature a broad cast of believable characters. Comedies stress physical humor, such as fistfights or pots of water thrown at characters.

In addition, the use of everyday speech further emphasized the increasing use of realism. This was not the witty dialogue, beautiful poetry, and clever wordplay that would later be perfected by Shakespeare and his contemporaries. Instead, the writers of the early Elizabethan period generally used dialogue that was spoken in rhymed couplets. This style is sometimes called "doggerel."

Perfecting the Space

By the early Elizabethan age acting had gradually become a viable profession, one at which a man could make a modest living. Furthermore, it was by now an entertainment that was enjoyed by the majority of people—both the general public and the nobility.

Most of these actors gravitated toward London, where there was the best chance of finding work. Some specialized in playing for the upper classes, especially in the royal court and the houses of the noble families. These performers and their audiences were generally well educated, acquainted with the classics of literature, and knowledgeable about new developments in theater in other countries.

At the same time, there were many groups of semiprofessional actors who specialized in performing for the general public. These troupes played wherever they could, charging admission or passing the hat to cover expenses. They eked out their precarious livings by setting up temporary stages in public squares, inns, or marketplaces. These stages were often nothing more than boards laid on top of barrels—the origin of a term for acting still used today, "treading the boards."

As the theater world became increasingly sophisticated, the physical spaces used by actors—the theaters themselves—grew equally sophisticated. This maturity developed in London.

The London Theaters

Since theatrical activity in England was centered in London, with little of consequence happening outside the capital, the history of Elizabethan theater is essentially that of the London theaters. These venues fell into two broad categories: open-air public theaters and smaller, more exclusive private theaters. Each had its own particular audience and style.

The physical layout and refinements of these theaters, while crude by today's standards, were major steps forward from the jury-rigged temporary stages that had served England's actors during the periods preceding the Elizabethan age. In the opinion of many, these were crucial steps without which the theatrical arts would not have blossomed. Theater historian Simon Trussler asserts, "The open-air 'public' playhouse, permanent and purpose-built, was the single innovation without which the so-called 'golden age' of the Elizabethan drama could scarcely have occurred."[14]

The First Theater

Some scholars believe that the first permanent public playhouse in London was a place called The Red Lion. However, there is no hard proof of this. It is generally acknowledged instead that the honor for the first permanent theater in England goes to a building called simply The Theatre. Whether or not The Theatre was really the first theater, it was certainly the first to house a significant resident acting company. It was the home of several important

A view of the interior of an open-air Elizabethan theater. These structures were the first permanent playhouses to be built in London.

companies of actors over the years, including Leicester's Men, The Admiral's Men, and The Lord Chamberlain's Men.

The Theatre was designed and built in 1576 by an actor, James Burbage. Burbage was then the head of a group of players called Leicester's Men. This troupe was so named in honor of their noble patron, the Earl of Leicester, an aristocrat who lent his prestige to the company.

Two years earlier Burbage had received an official blessing from Queen Elizabeth, in the form of an official license. It allowed him to work as an actor, to manage an acting troupe, and—crucially—to build a theater. This royal license was awarded to "a James Burbage and four fellows of the company of the Earl of Leicester to exhibit all kinds of stage-plays during the Queen's pleasure in any part of England." [15]

Regulating the Players

Acquiring such a license had just recently become important to actors. Until 1574 theatrical productions in England had been unregulated. They required no licenses or official permission, and anyone could mount a production anywhere and anytime. However, London's government changed all this in 1574. It passed a law requiring that all acting troupes be licensed. In addition, all individual plays were subject to censorship. An official, the Master of the Revels, was appointed to oversee these regulations.

The restrictive measures were enacted for several reasons. One was that plays were becoming increasingly bawdy. A politically powerful religious group, the Puritans, frowned on performances it considered sinful. More compelling was the fact that many plays were politically controversial. The authorities wanted to ensure that politically sensitive or slanderous material did not inflame the public. The city's leaders feared that plays with controversial themes had the potential to provoke rebellion.

Still another concern for the city fathers was the general issue of keeping the peace. Elizabethan audiences were notoriously rowdy and prone to fight. It was not uncommon for an audience to storm the stage of a play it did not like, or to riot among itself for no particular reason except that it liked a good battle.

More Concerns

Unlike their queen, who enjoyed the theater and tolerated the eccentricities of actors despite their status as commoners, London's authorities were mistrustful of actors and the rowdy audiences that followed them. Many of these city officials regarded drama as immoral, a wasteful pastime to be discouraged rather than tolerated. At one point the city's lord mayor proclaimed that plays were "a special cause of corrupting youth, containing nothing but unchaste matter, lascivious devices . . . and ungodly practices." [16]

On top of these concerns were two ever present and extremely practical considerations: the dangers of fire and plague. Fire was a constant hazard in a city of wooden

The threat of plague was ever-present in Elizabethan England. Here, the town crier calls on citizens to bring out their dead to be carried away on the cart in the background.

structures, and the authorities felt that any time a large group of people gathered, the danger of accidentally starting a blaze only increased. The plague was an even more terrifying prospect. London saw an average of forty to fifty deaths a week from this highly contagious disease during the Elizabethan era. The city's authorities wanted to have the power to ban crowds during a plague outbreak and thus enact a measure of control.

They did not succeed in shutting down the theaters entirely. They did, however, regularly close the theaters, sometimes for as long as two years at a stretch, in an attempt to control the spread of disease. In the winter of 1593, for example, during a particularly virile outbreak of the plague, the London Privy Council shut down the theaters for a long spell. Their proclamation banned "all plays, baiting of bears, bulls, bowling and other like occasions to assemble any number of people together (preaching and Divine Service excepted)." [17]

The Imitators

The strict London laws relating to theaters determined where Burbage built his structure. Eager to avoid the tight controls of the city authorities, he went outside the city limits to a northern suburb called Shoreditch. The Theatre was an immediate success, and it inspired a rash of imitators. J.L. Styan observes that the basic setup of The Theatre served as an excellent model for later enterprises: "The fact that it was used by other companies and exchanged

plays with other playhouses in its subsequent twenty years of life suggests that, in its rudiments, the formula suited everyone." [18]

Within months, and only a few streets away, a rival theater called The Curtain opened its doors. Its name came not from a theater curtain; such things were unknown then. Some sources say a family called Curtain owned the land, but probably the name derived from the French word *courtaine,* meaning a small courtyard.

Several other playhouses soon joined The Theatre and The Curtain. Among them were The Rose, The Red Bull, The Hope, The Fortune, and The Swan. In all, eight permanent public theaters were built in the London area in the thirty years after The Theatre's opening. At the same time, innumerable private or temporary performance spaces were also organized.

The practice of attending plays quickly became a regular routine for large numbers of Londoners from nearly all walks of life. Writer Christine Eccles notes, "By 1587, theatre had already evolved into a discrete [separate] and distinctive new art. London audiences in their thousands had supported [London's] playhouses [and] nothing— not plague, pickpockets nor the Puritan curse of everlasting damnation—was likely to break the habit." [19]

The Most Famous Theater

When James Burbage died in 1597 his sons Richard and Cuthbert inherited The Theatre. However, the lease on its land was

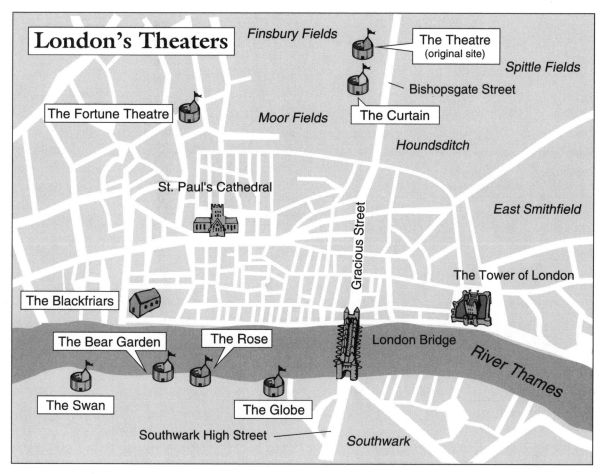

London's Theaters

Finsbury Fields

The Theatre (original site)

Spittle Fields

Bishopsgate Street

The Fortune Theatre

Moor Fields

The Curtain

Houndsditch

St. Paul's Cathedral

Gracious Street

East Smithfield

The Tower of London

The Blackfriars

The Bear Garden

The Rose

London Bridge

River Thames

The Swan

The Globe

Southwark High Street

Southwark

about to expire. Over the next two years, Richard and Cuthbert dismantled their play-house and recycled its timbers to build a new theater, The Globe.

When the Burbages built their new playhouse, they brought along The Lord Chamberlain's Men, the company of actors then resident at The Theatre. One member of this troupe was a rising young playwright and actor named William Shakespeare. Thanks to his many plays that debuted there, The Globe became the most famous of all Elizabethan theaters.

Its construction was probably finished in the autumn of 1599. This original Globe survived only until 1613, when it burned down in an accident. Thatch (dried straw often used for house roofs in Elizabethan England) formed a partial roof for the building, and this caught fire when a cannon was set off during a performance of Shakespeare's *Henry VIII*. The Globe was rebuilt on the same foundation and reopened in 1614.

The Theatre, London's first venue, had been located in the northern suburbs, but

A nineteenth-century depiction of two Elizabethan theaters (left and right). The actual appearance and design of Elizabethan theaters is a matter of scholarly debate.

when the Burbage brothers built The Globe they located it on the opposite south side of the River Thames, just west of London Bridge. This was a neighborhood called Bankside. Two theaters, The Swan and The Rose, already stood nearby.

Bankside was a rough neighborhood. It had long been a haven for tawdry public pleasures such as brothels, drinking-houses, and arenas devoted to bear- and bull-baiting. This grisly "sport" had been a favorite with Londoners since the days of the Romans who founded the town.

Many plays and other sources from the Elizabethan period refer to the fact that London's playhouses often doubled as arenas for such entertainment. When The Hope presented *Bartholomew Fair* as its opening production in 1614, the play's author, Ben Jonson, joked that the audience's leftover apples could be used as snacks for the bears.

Many Shapes, Same Basic Design

Evidence about how theaters like The Globe were built and what they looked like is somewhat limited. Writer Christine Eccles notes this lack of hard evidence when she comments, "Speculations and conjectures about Elizabethan playhouses form an industry in itself. Go into any library and shelves of books will say that Elizabethan playhouses had eight, twelve, twenty-four sides; that they were octagons, polygons, circles and polygons passing themselves off as circles."[20]

Nonetheless, historians have been able to reconstruct the typical public Elizabethan theater with a fair degree of accuracy. They base their conclusions on evidence such as surviving drawings and the physical remnants of The Rose, the foundation of which was discovered in Bankside in 1989.

According to this research, Elizabethan theaters generally had the same basic design, though they differed in details of size and shape. While their physical layout was not the extremely complex and sophisticated construction seen in theaters in later centuries, they were a far cry from the rough-hewn temporary stages England's actors had used earlier.

The centerpiece of each theater was a large platform, elevated about five feet off the ground. This served as the stage. Although some were enormous, the typical stage was only about forty feet square.

"This Wooden O"

There were also two separate areas for audience members. One was the large open area of ground that surrounded the stage on three sides. This section was called the yard or pit. Beyond the yard, rising on three sides to form the outside walls of the theater, was a three-storied wooden structure called the gallery. Like the yard, the gallery was a viewing area. It was more expensive, however, since audiences here enjoyed a better view of the stage and could sit instead of stand.

Depending on the individual theater, the gallery might take many shapes including round, square, or octagonal (eight-sided). Shakespeare refers to the shape of a theater in the prologue to his play *Henry V,* when he refers to dramatic action taking place within "this wooden O."

The gallery was roofed, usually with thatch or tile. Often, part of the stage was covered as well. However, the yard and most of the stage remained open to the elements, exposing audience members in the yard, and sometimes the actors as well, to England's notoriously rainy climate. In especially bad weather performances had to be canceled. A flag was hoisted above the theater to let audiences know if a show was on for a given day.

The open-air nature of public theaters also meant that plays could only be performed in the daytime, since candles or torches were not adequate to light the stages. Programs therefore took place in the afternoon. Two o'clock was a typical starting time.

Small but Packed

Elizabethan theaters were small compared to their modern-day equivalents. Excavations of The Rose, one of the smaller Elizabethan houses, indicate that its exterior diameter (measuring from the outside wall of the gallery) was about 74 feet, while its interior diameter was about 50 feet. The Globe was somewhat larger, with an exterior diameter of about 100 feet and an interior diameter of about 75 feet.

Despite these relatively small sizes, Elizabethan theaters could be packed with surprisingly large audiences. It has been estimated that as many as 2,500 to 3,000 people could attend a single performance. Not every performance was a sellout, however. One scholar has estimated, for instance, that during the year 1595 The Rose had an average daily attendance figure of about 1,250—that is, roughly half of full capacity.

In the basic architecture of their design, Elizabethan theaters tended to be rather plain and utilitarian. However, some of them were quite elaborately decorated in other ways. For instance, one observer wrote in 1598: "Of all the theatres, however, the largest and most distinguished is . . . The Swan, since it has space for 3,000 persons and is built of a concrete of flint stones, and supported by wooden columns, painted in such excellent imitation of mar-

Elizabethan theaters offered two separate areas to accommodate the audience: The pit, an open area before the stage where the lower classes stood, and the gallery, a three-storied wooden structure where upper-class patrons sat in comfort.

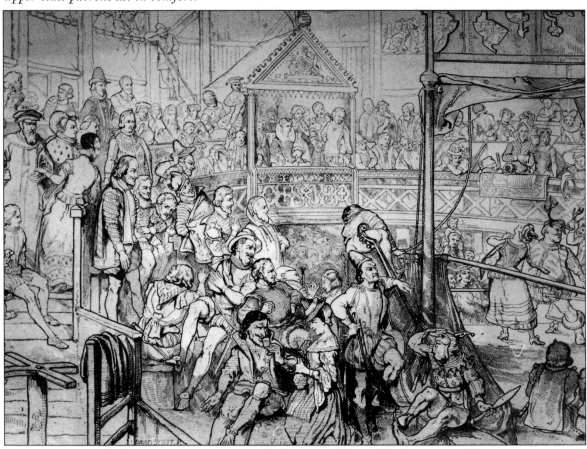

ble that it might deceive even the most prying."[21]

Behind the Facade

The typical Elizabethan theater stage was far more versatile than older forms of dramatic stages, such as amphitheaters from the Roman and Greek eras or the movable carts used for the medieval mystery plays. It could be used for many different types of dramas, and in many different ways. This newfound flexibility came from a combination of refinements and additions to the basic single platform.

The Romans and the Greeks in their amphitheaters and the performers of mystery cycles with their pageant wagons could do little on stage in terms of movement. Actors could only walk along the length of a narrow stage or perhaps move slightly toward or away from their audiences. In the Elizabethan era, however, it became possible for actors to move in many directions.

They could, for instance, use exits and the stage to move in a number of different directions relative to the audience and each other. More innovative, however, was the ability to go up and down—not just upstage and downstage, but literally up and down, perpendicular to the stage. This was possible because Elizabethan stages had a facade, a false front. The facade was at the rear of the stage. It formed the fourth side of the theater's walls as a continuation of the galleries on either side of it.

Facades had two or three levels. Doors at the stage level of the facade created the main entrance and exit points for actors.

Built into this level as well were several areas where actors could hide from the view of the audience. This made up in part for the fact that no curtain separated the stage from the audience to hide actors from public view between scenes.

Also on the stage level, hidden from public view, was a small room that could be curtained off and then opened during the course of a play. This was called the discovery room and was used for so-called discovery scenes. These were scenes in which an actor opened the curtain and "found" hidden characters, such as someone who had been eavesdropping on a secret conversation.

More Action Behind the Facade

Sometimes an actor performed in the discovery room with the curtain open. This allowed him to "hide" temporarily from other actors while remaining visible to the audience. If the curtain was left open in this way, a character hiding in the discovery room could be "unseen" by other actors on the main stage but remain perceived by the audience.

Located behind the stage level of the facade, hidden between the two doors that served as entrances and exits, was a small dressing room. This area was called the "tiring room," the name coming from the Elizabethan-era word for "attire."

Another small stage was built on the facade's second level. Actors could climb there, using interior stairs, if a scene required them to speak from a balcony,

Theater historian J.L. Styan points out that music was universal in the theater of the time. It provided entertainment, set a mood, and moved the drama forward: "During performance music could be all-pervasive. . . . Solemn or supernatural, pastoral or romantic, the music consciously assisted the work of the stage."[22]

Public Versus Private

The Globe, The Rose, and similar playhouses were known as public theaters. In addition to these, London had a number of venues known as private theaters. Among the most prominent of these were The Blackfriars, The Whitefriars, and The Salisbury Court. The Blackfriars was probably the first private theater. A prominent musician and theatrical producer, Richard Farrant, created it from an abandoned monastery near St. Paul's Cathedral in 1596.

In the case of private theaters, the term "private" is misleading, since these venues had many characteristics in common with public theaters. They used companies of professional actors, charged admission, and were open to the public. However, the owners and operators of private theaters worked hard to keep their theaters distinct from public theaters.

Private theaters were designed specifically to attract upper-class patrons: the wealthy, the noble, and the well educated. The plays these theaters featured were generally more formal, intellectual, and artificial than the boisterous, naturalistic plays enjoyed by audiences in public theaters.

Romeo embraces Juliet during the balcony scene in a modern production of Shakespeare's Romeo and Juliet.

wall, or other high place. Perhaps the most famous example of this is the balcony scene in *Romeo and Juliet*. Many theaters had a third level to the facade as well. This third level provided room for musicians to sit while playing during a performance.

A permanent space for musicians was a necessary part of any theater, because music was an essential part of Elizabethan drama.

Lights and Frames

Private theaters were also much smaller and more intimate than public theaters. The Blackfriars, for instance, was sixty-six feet by forty-six feet, with room for only about six hundred people seated on chairs. Private theaters, because they held fewer audience members, had to charge higher prices. Naturally, these more select audiences could afford higher fees.

Another difference was that the physical trappings of private theaters were generally more luxurious than public theaters. No one in the audience stood. Benches or chairs (on the level area in front of the stage) and raised galleries around the walls faced the stage, which was at one end of the building. Also, private theaters were all within roofed buildings. No one had to stand in the rain to see a play at a private theater.

Queen Elizabeth I is carried by her retinue to The Blackfriars, the first private theater in London. Private playhouses were devised to draw a more exclusive clientele than the public theaters.

In time, other elaborate ideas were incorporated into performances at private theaters. They were among the first venues in England where portable scenery was used. Later, in the early seventeenth century, private theaters also became the first theaters in England to incorporate the use of a proscenium arch. Borrowed from the Italian theater, which in turn had borrowed it from ancient Greek drama, this method of creating a visual "frame" around the stage is still a theatrical standard today.

Because private theaters were in enclosed and roofed spaces, performances could be put on at night. Candles were used to illuminate these evening performances; however, in order to be effective the candelabras were necessarily low-hanging. This probably created sight line problems for those audience members who were sitting in the galleries. For daytime performances, The Blackfriars, and probably other private theaters as well, had shuttered windows that offered a choice between natural and artificial light.

Other Refinements

The physical layout of London's theaters developed and improved tremendously during the Elizabethan era. No longer were actors working on temporary, poorly built stages. At the same time, other refinements were taking place in other aspects of the theatrical arts.

For one thing, actors were perfecting the ways in which they augmented their performances with stagecraft. Stagecraft—the use of theatrical devices and techniques—was reaching new heights of sophistication.

Between Heaven and Hell: Stagecraft

Compared to many modern productions, Elizabethan drama used relatively little stagecraft—that is, tools and techniques to augment the acting and help create theatrical illusions. There was almost no scenery, for example, and far fewer props than found in a typical modern production. Lighting, sound effects, and other techniques were likewise extremely limited.

Nonetheless, actors of the Elizabethan era used a much wider and more complex range of stagecraft than had their predecessors. Colorful costumes and other effects gave Elizabethan actors the power to amplify their illusions and transport audiences into different times and places.

This was especially true when the play called for lively action scenes such as battles, trials, and royal processions. Theater historian Alan Dessen notes that "most moments in Elizabethan productions involve only actors and a bare stage. But for major scenes or special occasions, large-scale, even spectacular, effects were possible."[23]

"Heaven"

As much as possible, Elizabethan actors used the physical spaces above, behind, and even below the stage. They took advantage of these spaces to augment and support the action on the main stage.

Theaters of the time typically covered at least part of the stage with a wooden or thatched roof. The underside of this roof was often painted like a night sky, with stars seeming to twinkle in the darkness. On top

41

of this roof, the theater's designers usually included a small hut. This hut was known as "Heaven" or "The Heavens."

Heaven was well suited to creating special effects. In particular, the magical, mystical appearance or disappearance of a character could be effected by mechanical means, using winches capable of lifting an actor from (or lowering him onto) the stage. Stagehands would be stationed in Heaven and, at the correct moment in the production, use the winches to bring the actor to or from "heaven on high."

Actors raised or lowered in this way were typically portraying deities. These gods and goddesses were frequent figures in Elizabethan plays. Often, their role was to appear unexpectedly and provide a solution to a thorny and otherwise unsolvable problem.

Such magical appearances by divine creatures had been common occurrences in ancient Greek and Roman drama as well as in miracle plays. The term for such intervention, "deus ex machina," is a Latin phrase meaning "god from (or out of) the machine." The phrase is still used today to refer to an unexpected savior or unlikely event that resolves a problem.

"Hell"

The opposite of Heaven, of course, was "Hell." This was the name given to the area beneath the raised stage in an Elizabethan theater. Since the stage was about five feet above the ground, there was plenty of room underneath in which to hide actors or store props.

Evocative costuming and authentic props contributed an air of reality to Elizabethan drama.

Actors used Hell in many ways. They could go behind the theater's facade, crawl under the stage, then make a sudden appearance onstage from a trapdoor that opened up into the stage. This trapdoor was a convenient entrance point for such supernatural apparitions as ghosts and devils, which were as common in Elizabethan drama as were gods and goddesses from above.

If left ajar, the trapdoor could also serve handily as an open grave. A famous example of this is the cemetery scene in Shakespeare's *Hamlet,* during which Hamlet, graveside, holds the skull of a royal jester and laments, "Alas, poor Yorick! I knew him, Horatio."

When an actor was hiding underneath the stage, he did not need to worry about exposure. Cloth hangings around the edges of the stage kept the goings-on in Hell from the eyes of anyone in the yard or galleries. These hangings were made in different colors and were changed according to the type of play being performed. Typically, black was used for tragedies, with red, white, or green generally preferred for comedies or histories.

"All Flies Up"

Heaven and Hell were not used only to bring gods and goddesses, or spirits and ghosts, in and out of the action. They were also handy areas from which to create an important but unseen part of Elizabethan performances: sound effects. For instance, stagehands could create the illusion of thunder by rolling cannonballs around on the floor of the hut above the stage. The sound of this "thunder" also conveniently served to hide the noise of Heaven's winches if they were lowering or raising an actor at the same time.

Processions, weddings, tournaments, the royal entertainments called masques, scenes of royal pomp—these were just some of the dramatic occasions during which actors could use special effects to enhance their show. Sometimes playwrights specified certain audio special effects. An example is "the noise of a sea-fight" called for in Shakespeare's *Antony and Cleopatra*. This effect was probably produced backstage or in Heaven by unseen stagehands.

Sometimes a play's writer left the addition of special effects unspecified. At other times the author added very precise directions for effects. In his play *The Silver Age*,

Hamlet soliloquizes while holding Yorick's skull in the cemetery scene of a recent production of Shakespeare's tragedy.

Thomas Heywood specified these stage directions at various points: "Enter Pluto with a club of fire, a burning crown . . . and a guard of Devils, all with burning weapons; Jupiter appears in his glory under a rainbow; Thunder, lightnings, Jupiter descends in his majesty, his thunderbolt burning; As he toucheth the bed it fires, and all flies up."[24]

Setting the Mood

Music, as always, played an important role. Trumpet blasts and drum rolls were common examples of music as sound effect. They typically signaled something of royal significance such as the entrance of a king or queen or the beginning of a battle. Trumpets served another role in the theater as well. They announced the play itself. Trumpet blares were used to let the audience know that the actors were ready to begin a play.

Elsewhere, music in general played a vital role in Elizabethan theater. Shakespeare and other writers of the era filled their plays, especially the comedies, with songs and dances. Instrumental music often accompanied these light interludes, but it was also used in other settings. For example, it could be used to set a certain mood. Shakespeare knew how well music can convey moods, and he often called for it to set the emotions of specific scenes. In his tragedy *Antony and Cleopatra,* for instance, he instructed that mysterious-sounding chords should be played before a scene depicting a fatal battle.

On occasion the special effects of the Elizabethan stage backfired. The original Globe Theatre, after all, had been destroyed by a fire that was caused by a cannon sig-

naling the appearance of the king during a performance of Shakespeare's *Henry VIII*.

No Scenery, Lots of Props

Unlike most modern plays, Elizabethan drama did not use portable painted backdrops—that is, scenery—to indicate the setting of the action onstage. The stage remained almost completely bare throughout the play. Historian Bernard Beckerman has analyzed all of the plays performed at The Globe between 1599 and 1609, and he concluded that 80 percent of the scenes in them "need nothing but a bare space and an audience, not so much as a stool."[25]

The lack of scenery allowed a play's action to flow freely from place to place. For example, the scenes in *Antony and Cleopatra* move smoothly between ancient Egypt and Rome and back again. Instead of lowering the curtain and changing scenery to create an illusion of changing time and place, Elizabethan plays could "quick-cut" from scene to scene as movies do today.

Since there was no scenery (and since, unlike modern plays, there were no programs to consult to know the setting of a scene), audiences did not know the setting of a play until the characters identified it through dialogue. However, Elizabethan dramatists made up for this lack of stage scenery in many ways, such as the frequent use of stage properties, or props. Props are items that actors use or handle during the course of a play.

A typical Elizabethan theater troupe amassed quite a collection of varied props to use over and over again in different

Antony (left) professes his abiding love for Cleopatra (seated) in a scene from a modern production of Shakespeare's tragedy Antony and Cleopatra.

productions. One inventory of a troupe's props, recorded in 1598, included the following: two steeples; a chime of bells; a beacon; a rock; a cage; a tomb; a "hellmouth" (entrance to hell); the city of Rome; the sun and the moon; the three heads belonging to Cerberus (the dog guardian of the River Styx in Greek mythology); a tree of golden apples; a huge horse with legs; and a cauldron.

Bladders of Pig's Blood and More

Many of the props used in Elizabethan productions were small, such as chairs, color-

ful banners, or swords. Actors could readily carry such props on- and offstage as they were needed. However, other props were too large and awkward to be handled with such ease. Typical of these larger props were fake fountains, trees, chariots, tombs, thrones and arbors (latticed shelters of shrubs or vines). Shakespeare's *Richard III*, for example, calls for two large tents, one at each end of the stage, to be erected onstage during a climactic battle scene.

Such large props had to be placed or removed by stagehands. It was necessary to do this, of course, in plain sight of the audience, since Elizabethan theaters had

45

no curtains. On occasion, even "dead" bodies had to be dragged off in this way.

Elizabethan actors also sometimes used hidden props, such as those for achieving the proper gory effects in a death scene. Theater historian James Roose-Evans writes, "The Elizabethans also had quite a taste for realistic death scenes, for tortures and mutilations on stage. The actor would carry a hidden bladder of pig's blood which would spout when pricked by dagger or rapier [short sword]. They also used animals' entrails [intestines] for display as was done in reality with human entrails by the executioner at Tyburn [Prison]."[26]

Costumes

Costumes were also a crucial element in Elizabethan stagecraft. They were among an actor's most treasured items. Theater historian Peter Thomson asserts, "Next to his [written] part, an actor's most precious possession was his costume."[27] Many Elizabethan plays require that actors play several roles, so the ability to race into the tiring room and change costumes quickly was crucial.

The better-established actors owned their own costumes, suitable for a variety of roles. They simply wore those if the role suited them. However, on many occasions the actors had to portray characters quite different from themselves, or quite different from their normal roles. Such roles might include nobility, divinities, or members of the opposite sex.

In such cases, more lavish or specialized costumes were required. These were typical-ly owned by the acting troupe as a group. Sometimes the troupe bore the cost of the costumes, and sometimes they were the gifts of wealthy patrons. Generally speaking, companies spent a great deal of time, money, and energy on their costume collections. They were beautifully designed, lovingly created, and carefully maintained.

Depending on its function, a costume might have been made of lush, brightly colored cloth and decorated with such flourishes as braid, embroidery, pearls, jewels, lace, or artificial flowers. Hats, perhaps decorated with feathers or jewels, were also important elements of any costume, since Elizabethan men generally wore hats everywhere, even indoors.

The Reasons Behind the Beautiful Clothes

There were several reasons why costuming was such an important, carefully prepared element of stagecraft. For one thing, the visual splendor of the actors' lavish costumes helped offset the lack of scenery and kept the stage from remaining colorless. Theater historian Peter Thomson writes, "The assumption that the Elizabethan stage was drab because it lacked elaborate scenery cannot be sustained. On the empty platform, costumes were individual splashes of colour and the composite picture was always vivid and could be splendid."[28]

Costuming—and any other aspect of stagecraft, for that matter—had to be particularly sumptuous if a troupe was invited to perform before royalty or nobility. Historian Ivor Brown notes, "It

Elizabethan actors used lavish costuming to help make portayals convincing, as in this scene from Shakespeare's A Midsummer Night's Dream, *in which Puck transforms Nick Bottom into an ass.*

is most unlikely that a Court audience, in which personal display with the height of masculine dandyism and feminine splendour was everywhere about, would put up with a naked stage or with actors playing the parts of Kings in garments obviously more suitable for the tag-rag commons." [29]

Sometimes even the most elaborate costuming could not cover up mediocre acting or writing. Furthermore, sometimes the costuming itself left much to be desired. A contemporary writer, Stephen Gosson, complained in 1582 that the romantic drama of the day was nothing "but the adventures of an amorous knight, passing from country to country for the love of his lady, encountering many a terrible monster made of brown paper." [30]

Identifying the Classes, Confusing the Genders

Perhaps the most important reason for emphasizing costumes was that it acted as a visual aid to the identification of characters. Audiences could immediately identify an actor's role by what he wore—an important factor, given the need to quickly establish who was who on stage. Audiences recognized characters by their dress because the differences between social classes and categories were very clearly marked in Elizabethan times.

People in certain occupations and classes always wore certain easily identifiable clothes. What a person wore thus immediately identified him or her by class and often by occupation as well. Given the proper visual clues, audiences could quickly recognize characters as doctors, merchants, king, craftsmen, or peasants, simply by what they wore. A queen and her lady-in-waiting, or a young woman and her nurse, also could be easily identified onstage.

Costuming also was important for an effect that was the opposite of clear identification—that of deliberate disguise. Elizabethan audiences in general loved disguises not only on the stage but for occasions such as masked balls, where one's identity could be hidden to thrilling effect. Disguise—usually achieved by a very simple costume change—is thus a common element in Elizabethan drama. A good example is the scene in Shakespeare's *Henry V,* where King Henry dons a hooded cloak in order to move undetected among his men on the eve of a major battle.

The Elizabethans also loved plays that created comic situations in which the sexes were mixed up, resulting in a delicious form of gender confusion. Many comedies of the era feature situations in which a female character is forced to disguise herself as a man. Female characters masquerade as men in

several of Shakespeare's best-known plays, including *As You Like It* and *The Merchant of Venice.* This deliberate confusion of genders was heightened by the fact that all Elizabethan actors were male. It was thus a common occurrence to have a man portraying a woman portraying a man.

The Masque

The most elaborate use of costumes and props in Elizabethan drama was in a phenomenon that was not strictly a play, but which was related and which had a major influence on the development of theater of the time. This unusual form of drama was called the masque or court masque.

Masques were elaborate theatrical presentations, performed one time only before a royal or noble audience. They generally began with elaborate dances performed by the court's lords and ladies. These nobles were masked and costumed for the occasion as such figures as shepherds or characters from history or mythology.

At some point in the evening, professional actors performed a drama related to the event's theme. This usually had some mythological, allegorical, or symbolic point carefully designed to cast the evening's hosts in a positive light. These dramatic portions of the performance involved still more lavish costumes along with splendid scenery, elaborate machinery to move it on- and offstage, and rich spoken verse.

Masques usually ended when the performers invited members of the royal audience, who were still costumed, to join them in a further series of dances. Afterwards, all

In this scene from a modern production of Shakespeare's As You Like It, *Rosalind (left) is disguised as a man in order to test the love of Orlando (center). Confusion of genders was a commonly used device in Elizabethan drama.*

participants—royal, noble, and actors—removed their masks and mingled together.

Highly Cultivated Memory

The masque had developed elsewhere in Europe, where variations on this form of royal entertainment were known by such names as "intermezzo" or *trionfo* (in Italy) and "masquerade" or *ballet de cour* (in France). Henry VIII, Elizabeth's father, witnessed these productions during his time abroad and introduced them to England.

Henry loved dancing and theatrical shows, and he instructed that similar events be held regularly in his court. Elizabeth continued the tradition, and under her reign the masque reached new levels of lavishness and perfection. Like her father, Elizabeth loved extravagant entertainment, and she was always ready to dance. Finely worded and acted plays or masques were very pleasing to her.

She also appreciated beautiful examples of the art of rhetoric, or public speaking. Writer Christine Eccles notes that such appreciation was typical of Elizabethan England: "Memory was highly cultivated. Public speaking, as an art, was emphasised. The Queen herself was an acknowledged star performer at highly competitive set orations." [31]

49

Ironically for a period of history when women were forbidden to act on a stage, Queen Elizabeth was herself widely regarded as a great performer in the masques held in her honor. In these she usually portrayed one of a variety of classical or biblical figures such as Deborah, Judith, Diana, Cynthia, or Gloriana.

Honoring the Queen

Elizabeth was a frugal queen, however. She did not like to spend money on entertainment. She preferred instead to witness plays and masques mounted by others in her honor. These entertainments were generally presented to the queen by her loyal subjects at court or during her annual summer tours through England.

An example of such a royal performance was the masque presented before Elizabeth in 1595 by the gentlemen of Gray's Inn, one of the institutions associated with London's law universities. Its story involved the Prince of Purpoole (invented

Players perform for Queen Elizabeth I (seated on throne) and her court. Such private performances were regularly given in the queen's honor.

for the occasion) and Proteus, who in classical mythology was the old man of the sea who could change his shape. The allegorical or symbolic aspect of the play takes shape by indirectly celebrating the glory of Elizabeth. A contest is set up between Proteus (representing a changeable nature) and the Prince (representing the loyal devotion of the inn's members to their queen). Naturally, the forces loyal to the queen are triumphant.

Performances of masques such as this one evolved into pageants of truly gigantic proportions, especially in the later part of Elizabeth's reign and the years after her death. They involved extravagant costumes, elaborate disguise, and complex, custom-built props and scenery.

Influencing Everyday Theater

Many of the inventions and refinements of stagecraft originally developed for masques eventually found their way into public theaters and had a strong influence on them. Generally speaking, the masque form was responsible for an increasingly heavy emphasis in Elizabethan theater on pomp, pageantry, and elaborate costuming.

One of these refinements was the use of a concealing front curtain pioneered by the Elizabethan designer Inigo Jones, one of the primary forces behind the development of elaborate royal masques.

The curtains concealed the use onstage of special machines Jones had designed. These machines created such illusions as landscapes, mountains, and castles that magically transformed into one another. The curtain as well as modified versions of Jones's machinery and other elaborate effects soon found their way into public performances and theaters. The use of a curtain remains standard practice in theaters today.

As the stagecraft of the theater became more fully developed, the writing of plays continued to flower and become richer. Elizabethan playwrights were usually under great pressure, quickly cranking out endless successions of tragedies, histories, and comedies. Nonetheless, they managed to create some of the most beautiful and enduring works in the English language.

Chapter 5

Ordinary Poets: Elizabethan Playwrights

Writing for the theater was in many ways an unpromising career for an Elizabethan. Historian Scott McMillin asserts, "When Shakespeare first came to London and began writing for a living, he took up the least respectable, riskiest, and potentially most profitable medium—the common stage."[32] The theater was not considered an honorable occupation—and if theater folk were disreputable, writers were some of the lowest on the theater ladder. Among writers in general, theater writers were held in low esteem; poetry was where the honor lay.

Elizabethan Screenwriters

For most playwrights the financial rewards were limited. Playwrights sold their work outright to theater troupes, usually for only a small amount of money. They received no royalties. On top of that, there was little public recognition of writers. Even a star like Shakespeare was not usually the name to be reckoned with when a new production was mounted. The lead actor was the person that audiences recognized and clamored to see.

On the other hand, the potential for profit was high for those willing to take a risk. In many ways, including this willingness to risk, Elizabethan playwrights resembled today's Hollywood screenwriters. As with a screenwriter, the chance of making money was slim for an Elizabethan playwright—but a small fortune awaited a successful writer.

Like screenwriters, Elizabethan playwrights turned out material quickly under great pressure, often collaborating with other writers. They also had to mold their works to the demands of many others including censors, producers, and actors. This forced them to become even more collaborative. In exchange, playwrights received the privilege of working in an exciting, stimulating environment. They expanded the horizons of a quickly developing and relatively new medium. And, of course, they could hope for some money.

Speed Writing

Playwrights were under constant pressure to work fast because the need for a steady stream of new material was tremendous. To meet this demand, many dramatists simply retooled old plots into new plays that met current fashions. Elizabethan audiences liked revivals of old favorites, but they loved to see new plays even more. A popular troupe might have a dozen plays in its repertoire at any given time, constantly dropping old ones in favor of new arrivals.

It was not customary in those days to give plays extensive runs. A play was normally performed only once; a run of three or four performances indicated a smash hit. Playwrights therefore were always in a hurry to complete the current project and get on with the next.

Writers collaborated frequently to satisfy the need for speed. One scholar has estimated that at least 20 percent of Elizabethan plays include a contribution from more than one writer. Producer Philip Henslowe's diaries suggest that only one-third of the plays presented by his troupes were the work of a single playwright.

Three, four, or even five dramatists working on a single play was not unusual. Theater historian Christine Eccles notes, "As only two or three weeks sometimes elapsed between taking the idea [for a play] to the company and bringing back to them the completed script, a team of writers was necessary to fulfill the punishing schedule." [33]

A portrait of William Shakespeare. Because Elizabethans held playwrights in low regard, the Bard's decision to write plays was a risky one.

Differing Speeds

Judging by what we know of overall production, a rate of two or three plays per year seems typical. Only one contract pertaining to a dramatist still exists from Elizabethan times. It stipulated that the dramatist write two plays per year.

However, playwrights differed greatly in their production. Shakespeare averaged twice the typical number, while Ben Jonson sometimes took two years to complete a single play. Thomas Heywood, one of the era's most prolific writers, claimed to have had at least a part in the creation of 220 plays during his long career.

The contrasts among writers and their speed of production could be extreme.

A portrait of Ben Jonson. In an era in which playwrights produced an average of two plays per year, Jonson sometimes needed two years to complete a single work.

Theater historian Carol Rutter has pointed this out by comparing two playwrights at work for producer Philip Henslowe in the summer of 1598:

> [George] Chapman at thirty-eight years of age was something of a donkey, content to plod along, solitary, while the young veteran Thomas Dekker (only twenty-six) was the stable's sociable farmyard cock, perpetually scratching around for more work. The same month Chapman was working on a single play, and finding it difficult to produce even a title for it, Dekker was involved in six plays, all of them collaborations.[34]

Ordinary Poets

Some playwrights were closely associated with particular troupes of players or even under contract to them—a position that today would be called a "resident dramatist." The term in Elizabethan times was "ordinary poet."

Some writers were full members of acting troupes and so shared in the profits. However, many ordinary poets were essentially just paid employees. Many others were freelancers who simply tried to sell their wares to whichever company would have them. Historian Thomas Whitfield Baldwin notes that a typical Elizabethan playwright "was not the master of the company but the servant."[35]

Even if a writer was only a salaried employee or a freelancer, there was the potential for making a good living. A top playwright could make six to ten pounds for a finished script, more than a cloth maker made in an entire year. Historian Scott McMillin notes, "The actors paid writers a better wage than did the Church, the university, the grammar school, or the noble family." [36]

Only a few writers were paid enough to survive on producing for the theater. Many had to supplement their income with other forms of writing, by acting, or by such nontheatrical methods as gambling. These extracurricular activities often got writers into trouble; occasionally producers had to pay off writers' debts, deducting this money from future payments. Philip Henslowe, for instance, recorded that early in 1598 he bailed writer Thomas Dekker out of jail for two pounds. Henslowe settled the debt by paying Dekker a mere four pounds for his next play, *Phaeton*.

Typically, a writer would read a few pages of a work in progress to a troupe of actors, who would pay him to complete it (or keep a salaried writer on the project) if it seemed promising. On one occasion in 1599, Henslowe authorized the payment of three pounds "to bye a boocke [play] called the Gentle Craft of Thomas Dickers [Dekker]." [37]

On another occasion in 1601 actor Samuel Rowley wrote to Henslowe urging him to approve a play: "Mr. Henslowe, I have heard five sheets of a play of the Conquest of the Indies and I do not doubt but it will be a very good play; therefore I pray you to deliver them [the writers] forty shillings in earnest of it and take the papers

The Roaring Girle.
OR
Moll Cut-Purse.

As it hath lately beene Acted on the Fortune-stage by the Prince his Players.

Written by T. Middleton and T. Dekker.

My case is alter'd, I must worke for my liuing.

Printed at London for Thomas Archer, and are to be sold at his shop in Popes head-pallace, neere the Royall Exchange. 1611.

The title page for the original edition of Thomas Middleton's and Thomas Dekker's The Roaring Girl. *Elizabethan plays were rarely published during the author's lifetime.*

into your own hands, and on Easter Eve they promise to make an end of all the rest." [38]

Publishing

Elizabethan plays were almost never published during the lives of their writers. Sometimes they were not published until many years after the authors had died. In part, this was because authors worried about other writers stealing their plays; unlike today, there were no copyright laws protecting writers from plagiarism. Also, many writers simply did not think their plays were worth preserving. Shakespeare, for one, considered his poetry far more important than the plays he dashed off for money. In his opinion the poems were his lasting legacy, while the plays were simply popular entertainment.

Because of this casual attitude toward printing plays, published Elizabethan plays are in most cases not exact records of what the authors wanted. They are not careful stage directions and exact dialogue. Instead, they are vague records of what once took place on a stage, often simply reconstructed from an actor's memory. Among the exceptions are the plays of Ben Jonson, who took care to see that his works were properly published during his lifetime.

On those occasions when Elizabethan plays were published, they typically came in two forms: anthologies of several plays, called folios, or smaller single-play editions, called quartos. Many different editions of the most popular plays have been published over the years, and these different versions have various degrees of accuracy. The differences among versions of Shakespeare's plays, for instance, have made it difficult for scholars to create authoritative versions.

Practical Considerations

Many practical considerations affected the ways in which Elizabethan playwrights worked. One factor was the advice of the actors for whom it was created. Typically, the playwright read the first act of a new play to his troupe as soon as it was finished. The actors then offered suggestions and criticism, and the writer revised accordingly.

During rehearsal, the writer revised yet again to smooth out rough edges. In *Hamlet,* Shakespeare uses this process of suggesting changes in scenes and dialogue as part of the plot. A crucial moment in the story involves Prince Hamlet writing an extra scene into a play that is shown before the royal family, as a trap for his murderous stepfather.

The rise in popularity of private theaters was another factor affecting the way in which writers produced their work. Playwrights writing for private theaters needed to alter their styles to suit wealthier and more sophisticated audiences. The result was a more refined style than plays written for public theater consumption.

Since playwrights almost always wrote for specific troupes, the strengths of individual performers also determined the writing. Comic performers were always popular and so were written into even the most somber plays. Shakespeare's *King Lear* is a good example. One of the bleakest of tragedies, it nonetheless has a juicy role for a comic performer—the king's fool.

Genres and Blank Verse

Elizabethan playwrights generally followed certain conventions, or standard practices. One of the most characteristic is the use of certain categories or genres. Elizabethan plays roughly fall into one of three genres: history, comedy, or tragedy. Comedies were by far the most popular in their day, outnumbering tragedies by about three to one.

A scene from a recent production of Shakespeare's King Lear. *Lear defies the elements during a storm while the fool provides comic relief by cowering beneath his robes.*

Some Elizabethan writers mixed the genres, however, making it difficult to categorize plays that have strong elements of more than one. Scholars differ, for instance, on whether Shakespeare's *Julius Caesar* is a tragedy or a history. A similar ambiguity concerns *Romeo and Juliet*'s classification—is it a romance or a tragedy?

Shakespeare himself made fun of these hybrid forms in *Hamlet*. One of the play's characters, Polonius, praises a visiting troupe of performers and describes them as "the best actors in the world, either for tragedy, comedy, history, pastoral, pastoral-comical, historical-pastoral, tragical-historical, tragical-comical-historical-pastoral." [39]

Another common convention concerned language. Prior to the Elizabethan period most English plays were written in rhymed couplets (successions of two rhymed lines). By the Elizabethan era, however, a new, mostly unrhymed style was taking hold.

Blank verse, as it was called, was developed by Italian poets of the early Renaissance, who based it on Greek and Latin poetry. They felt it closely approximated the natural rhythms of speech. The style gradually became the dominant form for all European poetry and drama, including Elizabethan theater.

The rhythm used in blank verse is called iambic pentameter. In poetry, an "iamb" is one unstressed syllable followed by one long or stressed syllable, such as the word "because." "Pentameter" refers to five of these syllable pairs. An example of iambic pentameter is the opening line of Shakespeare's *Twelfth Night:* "If music be the food of love, play on." [40]

The University Wits

Many scholars consider Shakespeare's work the high point of Elizabethan drama. However, many important writers created their primary works just before or during Shakespeare's time. The first wave of playwrights who might be considered true Elizabethans emerged in the 1580s and

A portrait of Thomas Dekker, a member of a group of playwrights known as the University Wits who rose to prominence in the 1580s and 90s.

1590s. This loose group, known as the University Wits, included John Lyly, Thomas Dekker, and Thomas Kyd.

The group was dubbed the University Wits because all of them were well educated, skilled at using classical references in their work, and accomplished poets as well as playwrights. Their work, intellectual and refined, appealed primarily to the educated and wealthy classes.

The plays of writers such as Lyly, Dekker, and Kyd do not show the maturity of later works, however. Their plots and characters tend to be simple and one-sided. Furthermore, the dialogue is still in rhymed couplets, not blank verse. Nonetheless, their plays were excellent preludes to the full flowering of Elizabethan writing, combining classical styles with the rough-and-ready, audience-pleasing traditions of popular entertainment.

Spell of the Sea God

John Lyly's comedy *Galathea,* written about 1585, skillfully uses advanced techniques in dialogue and plot construction. It also makes the most of the ever popular devices of sexual confusion and deus ex machina. In it, a fictional country is under the spell of the sea god Neptune, who must be appeased by sacrificing a maiden to a sea monster. Two men dress their daughters up as boys in an attempt to save them, but the disguised girls fall in love with each other. Venus, the goddess of love, then intervenes, turning one of the girls into a boy so that the two can marry.

Dekker was skilled at incorporating everyday life into his plays. Typical is *The Shoemakers Holiday, or The Gentle Craft* (1599). It weaves a portrait of everyday life around love stories of ordinary people, not gods or fairies, and the saga of a shoemaker, Simon Eyre, who rises in the world through luck, industry, and high spirits. According to theater historians Parrott and Ball, "It would be hard to find another Elizabethan play where the background of contemporary life gives so strong a sense of atmosphere, an atmosphere of Old and Merry England at its jolliest."[41]

Thomas Kyd's *The Spanish Tragedie*, written about 1590, was one of the first English plays written in blank verse. It is also an early example of the so-called tragedy of revenge, in which an evil act is bloodily avenged. The play's hero, Hieronimo, seeks justice for the murder of his son, finds it can be achieved only when he takes the law into his own hands, and suffers tragic consequences.

Marlowe

The careers of the University Wits overlapped somewhat with those of three writers considered by many to be the greatest of the Elizabethan Age. These men were Christopher Marlowe, Ben Jonson, and William Shakespeare.

Today Christopher Marlowe is remembered most for the depth and vigor of his tragic characters, his brilliant use of language, and the bold pageantry he brought to the stage. His plays were intellectually challenging; they addressed the deep questions of his time, questions created by the Renaissance's rapid changes in politics, commerce, and science.

Theater historians Parrott and Ball argue that Marlowe's refinement of blank verse was his most important contribution to the theater. They write, "It is not too much to say that this noblest of all English verse forms is essentially the creation of Christopher Marlowe. Shakespeare was to expand its range, but in this, as in so much else, Marlowe was the master from whom Shakespeare learned the secret of his art."[42]

Marlowe's heroes are strong but tragic figures whose towering ambitions lead to their downfall. One example is his first major success, *Tamburlaine the Great* (1587), which was inspired by the legendary Mongol warrior Timur. Another well-known example is *The Tragicall History of Dr. Faustus* (1604), based on the old German story of a man who sells his soul to the Devil.

A scene from a modern production of Christopher Marlowe's The Tragicall History of Dr. Faustus. *Faustus (right) prepares to sell his soul to the Devil.*

The playwright's reputation during his lifetime was great—probably even greater than that of his chief rival, Shakespeare. However, his career was tragically short. Arrogant and supremely self-confident, Marlowe led a turbulent life that included imprisonment for homicide; he died at age twenty-nine after being stabbed in a tavern brawl.

A Comedian of "Humours"

Another outstanding writer of the era was Ben Jonson. He specialized in satire, that is, making fun of something. His comedies satirizing such universal human failings as greed, ignorance, foolishness, and superstition are still performed today.

Jonson's fame came with a style of comedy called the comedy of humours. In medieval times a commonly held medical concept was that good health depended on a balance of four humours, or bodily fluids: blood, phlegm, yellow bile, and black bile. An excess of one supposedly dominated a person's disposition; too much bile, for example, made one melancholy.

By Elizabethan times, "humours" referred simply to individual temperaments or whims. The seventeenth century poet John Dryden defined these as "some extravagant habit, passion, or affection, particular . . . to some one person, by the oddness of which he is immediately distinguished from the rest of men." [43]

Jonson's comedies of humours portrayed eccentric characters who emphasized such traits. *Volpone, or The Foxe* (1606), is often regarded as Jonson's masterpiece.

Although set in Venice, the play clearly satirizes the rising merchant class of London.

Like many Elizabethan playwrights, Jonson led a tumultuous life. Among other adventures, he narrowly escaped hanging for killing an actor in a duel. Producer Philip Henslowe, sarcastically referring to Jonson's former profession, noted that he had sustained a serious loss "which hurteth me greatley," and mourned the actor, "slayen . . . by the handes of bengemen Jonson bricklayer." [44]

A Towering Genius

During his life Marlowe was probably the best-known playwright in England. Meanwhile, for nearly one hundred years after his death, Jonson was considered the greatest playwright of his time. In the years since, however, one man's name has become virtually synonymous with Elizabethan theater. To many, William Shakespeare is not only the greatest of the Elizabethan playwrights, and not only the greatest dramatist who wrote in English, but the greatest dramatist of all time and in any language.

Strictly speaking, Shakespeare did not contribute much that was entirely new. He did not invent blank verse, and he refined dramatic techniques that earlier playwrights had introduced rather than inventing new ones. Furthermore, he freely borrowed from many sources for his plots, including fiction, histories, myths, and earlier plays.

Nonetheless, Shakespeare remains unequaled in his ability to write rich dialogue, create deep characters, and relate human experience to universal philosophi-

William Shakespeare (kneeling) performs on stage. Shakespeare began his theater career as an actor and a prompter.

cal questions. No other playwright has been produced, read, or quoted more often. Most serious actors and actresses consider the major Shakespearean roles to be the supreme test of their art.

A Life in the Theater

Shakespeare began his dramatic career as an actor and a prompter, someone who helps other actors speak their lines if they forget them onstage. He rose steadily in the London theater world, however, and by about 1594 was a key member of the top acting troupe in London, The Lord Chamberlain's Men.

Most of his plays were premiered by this troupe at The Globe. Records are scanty, and it is impossible to date Elizabethan plays precisely, though there is a general consensus about the debut performances of Shakespeare's early plays. In rough order, they include *Henry VI, Parts I, II, and III* (1589–1592); *Richard III* and *The Comedy of Errors* (1592–1593); *Titus Andronicus* and *The Taming of the Shrew* (1593–1594); *The Two Gentlemen of Verona, Love's Labour's Lost,* and *Romeo and Juliet* (1594–1595).

During his most productive years Shakespeare wrote a mixture of histories and comedies. Tragic elements in such plays as *Richard III* and *Romeo and Juliet,* however, indicated how Shakespeare would occupy his next years: by writing his great tragedies, including *Hamlet* and *King Lear.*

As a partner in The Lord Chamberlain's Men, Shakespeare was able to share in the company's profits. As their popularity grew, and because he held shares in The Globe, he became a wealthy man. He died just shy of his fifty-second birthday in his home town, Stratford-upon-Avon.

Even a writer of genius like Shakespeare, however, was not the star in a troupe of Elizabethan players. Writers were not held in high esteem by audiences, and announcements advertising new plays often did not even mention the writers' names. (As an actor, Shakespeare was not a big star.) The primary attractions for typical Elizabethan audiences remained the actors.

Treading the Boards: Actors

The playwrights who created Elizabethan drama did not work alone, of course. They needed people to translate their words from the page to the stage. This was the job of the actor.

The actor, at least in the opinion of the typical audience member, was the most important element in creating a successful play. Theater historian Peter Thomson notes, "It was less often the playwright whose name attracted audiences (playbills seem not to have mentioned it), than the reputation of the actors, who had bought the plays as commodities and laboured to turn them into profitable merchandise." [45]

The top actors were therefore much-praised and admired stars. One contemporary writer, Thomas Nashe, commented about the actor Edward Alleyn that none of "those admyred tragedians that haue liued euer [have lived ever] since before Christ was borne, could euer perform more in action than famous Ned Alleyn." [46]

Virtuosos of the Stage

It is not clear how many plays were produced in London during an average theater season. However, surviving records for one prominent troupe provide a glimpse into what may have been a typical year. During the late 1590s The Admiral's Men performed thirty to forty plays a year, around half of them new. They typically gave six performances every week over a season lasting more than forty weeks.

The constant appearance of new works was all important to a troupe's continued success and popularity. During one ten-week period in 1595, for example, The Admiral's Men gave fifty-seven performances of twen-ty different plays, four of them new. Peter Thomson writes, "Nothing is clearer . . . than that new work brought bigger audiences, that novelty was short-lived and that any play performed six or more times in a season was an exceptional success."[47]

Mounting so many plays left no time for long rehearsals. Actors had perhaps only three weeks in which to prepare a given play, memorizing parts for many different plays at a time, often with more than one role per play. A busy Elizabethan actor might have had as many as fifty different parts in twenty-five different productions within a single month.

Taking on multiple roles in a single play is called doubling. It was not necessarily done to save the troupe money. Often, actors regarded doubling as a matter of professional pride. Theater historian Scott McMillin writes, "Doubling belonged to the actors' craft. Along with being elocutionists [fine speakers] and acrobats, they were quick-change artists, and part of the pride of a good performer was his ability to play quite different kinds of roles on a single afternoon."[48]

How Elizabethan actors learned all these lines so quickly is something of a mystery to modern historians. McMillin further comments:

The memories of Elizabethan actors are among the unexplained phenomena of human history—these were not short plays; the dialogue was among the most complex poetry ever written for the stage; there was nothing but

A portrait of Edward (Ned) Alleyn, a famous Elizabethan actor.

candle light to work from at night; you could not know what the other roles consisted of while you learned yours; and on Sundays the preacher would be telling everyone you were doing something immoral.[49]

Quick Talkers

Despite the virtuoso amount of memorization required, it appears that Elizabethan actors always spoke very clearly and musically. Evidence also indicates that they spoke their lines more quickly than the typical modern performer. This fits in with another assumption made by modern scholars: that there was very little time during a play when no one was speaking onstage. Getting through, say, a five-act tragedy in a few hours would require plenty of rapid speech and not much of what actors now call "silent business."

An actor's speaking style had to be extremely distinct and lucid for several reasons. One, of course, was that everyone in the theater had to hear the actors clearly without amplification. Also, Elizabethan audiences simply appreciated fine oratory.

Audiences were also notorious for making their opinions known, and an actor with anything less than rapid but lucid diction would surely have been booed off the stage. Writer Robertson Davies points out, "Rapidity of speech without skill would certainly have provoked those temperamental audiences to bitter comment. . . . The great actor was a virtuoso and the audience expected a brilliant display of his powers."[50]

Elizabethan audiences were extremely vocal, and were quick to ridicule poorly written plays or to boo mediocre actors from the stage.

"Heavilie" and "Sad"

Acting requires far more than simply speaking one's lines well. Players also needed to develop full-bodied characters capable of expressing a range of emotions, using only speech, a few gestures, and a minimum of props. The Elizabethans called this process "personation," which writer Peter Thomson defines as "the making concrete of something so intangible as an invented personality."[51]

As far as modern historians can tell, actors needed to develop this ability on their own. They apparently had few specific

Actor Steven Berkoff as Hamlet in a 1980 stage production. Berkoff's face demonstrates the Elizabethan process of personation, *developing a character's range of emotions.*

written cues from playwrights telling them how to play a particular scene. If such cues did exist, they were generally limited to one-word descriptions such as "heavilie" or "sad."

Elizabethan actors developed "short-hand" ways of quickly conveying these moods or emotions to their audiences. Robertson Davies notes,

In a theatre where new plays were constantly being presented there would be little time to do more than learn the words of a part and have a few rehearsals, which would give slight opportunity for

elaborate training in individual roles. . . . There were no doubt well-worn gestures for contempt, rage, pity, remorse, and all the other emotions, which the audience would quickly accept as symbols of them.[52]

Soliloquies, Asides, and More

Actors could quickly show an audience a character's emotion through two common conventions that developed during the Elizabethan period—the soliloquy and the aside. In a soliloquy, an actor who is alone onstage recites a long speech directly to the audience or speaks his thoughts and feelings aloud "to himself." An aside is a brief comment made by a character, speaking words that other characters onstage are not supposed to hear.

Unlike modern actors, Elizabethan players never had complete scripts to work from when preparing their roles. Since companies were eager to avoid having their new works pirated by rival troupes, the full text of a new play was a closely guarded treasure. Usually only a single "book" (the full version of a play) was entrusted to one man.

This man, called the Book-keeper, used the master copy to prepare separate copies that contained only the lines of individual actors, with a few preceding lines included to cue him. The Book-keeper then handed these individual sections out to each actor.

In order to help the actors keep things straight, the Book-keeper posted a written outline of the plot backstage so that the players could use it as a memory aid during performances. He also served as a prompter during performances, sitting backstage near an opening through which he could watch, hear, and speak if an actor forgot his lines.

The Top Troupes

Though the top professional actors were all based in London, a handful of troupes operated outside the city, endlessly touring small towns and villages. These groups were often ridiculed by the more polished Londoners. Thomas Dekker commented disdainfully that such players "travel upon the hard hoofe from village to village for chees & buttermilke." [53]

They were unable to perform in the capital because London theater had become a virtual monopoly. The number of troupes operating in the city was strictly controlled, with no more than five professional troupes allowed to operate at a given time. Each of these troupes was required to have an official license issued by the master of the revels. These authorized troupes regularly dissolved, formed, and reformed, with members often moving from one to the other. Nonetheless, two troupes lasted for years with relatively stable membership.

One was The Lord Chamberlain's Men, which boasted William Shakespeare as its "ordinary poet" as well as several outstanding performers. Chief among these was the gifted tragedian Richard Burbage, for whom many of Shakespeare's best and most challenging roles were custom-tailored. The Lord Chamberlain's Men had a further advantage in The Globe, considered by many to be the best public theater in the city.

The closest rivals to The Lord Chamberlain's Men were The Admiral's Men, also called The Lord Admiral's Men. The most famous "ordinary poet" associated with this troupe was Christopher Marlowe, and its manager was financier-manager Philip Henslowe. The troupe's outstanding dramatic actor, Edward Alleyn, was also Henslowe's son-in-law and business partner.

The Funny Men

In addition to the serious roles favored by actors such as Burbage and Alleyn, comedy was an important part of Elizabethan theater.

It was so important, and so consistently popular, that comic scenes were inserted into even the most violent of histories or the saddest of tragedies. The first gravedigger in *Hamlet* and the porter in *Macbeth* are examples of comic characters who appear in otherwise somber tragedies.

Some actors gravitated toward comedy and made it their specialty. For many years the leading comic actor in The Lord Chamberlain's Men was Will Kempe. As he did with leading romantic or tragic roles, Shakespeare created comic characters that specifically reflected the strengths of an actor such as Kempe. The comic roles in such comedies as *A Midsummer Night's Dream* and *Much Ado About Nothing* were thus customized for the broad humor typical of Kempe's acting, singing, and dancing.

After Kempe left the company in 1599, Robert Armin took his place, and the style of Shakespeare's writing shifted. Armin had more sophisticated and intellectual comic talents; his strength was in playing characters who were sharp-tongued and wise, sometimes with a bittersweet turn. These characteristics were used to great advantage

Will Kempe (right), a comic actor in a troupe known as The Lord Chamberlain's Men, performs a folk dance called the Morris.

in the more thoughtful comedies Shake-speare wrote later in his career, such as *Twelfth Night,* as well as such roles as the fool in the bleak tragedy *King Lear.*

Another famous clown was William Rowley, who probably began his career with Queen Anne's Men and achieved fame with The King's Men. Rowley was a large man, and usually appeared in roles that took advantage of his girth, such as Plumporridge in *The Inner Temple Masque* and the Fat Bishop in *A Game at Chaess* (both written by Thomas Middleton). In a play Rowley wrote, *All's Lost by Lust,* the portly actor created the role of "Fat Clown" for himself.

Apprentices

Women were banned from appearing on the Elizabethan stage. Instead, adult males portrayed older women, and boy actors took the roles of young females. Robertson Davies points out that this practice was the continuation of a very old custom: "The tradition of boy actors in England extends from the beginnings of drama in the Middle Ages, when church liturgy fathered the mystery and morality plays, and the choir-boys assisted the clerks in their presentation." [54]

Usually, three to five boys belonged to a troupe at any given time. Boys were usually apprenticed to acting troupes between the ages of six and fourteen but probably did not appear onstage before the age of twelve or so. Until then, they were kept busy running errands, such as fetching props for the stage master. Many of them went on to become full-fledged adult actors.

Besides an apprenticeship with a regular acting troupe, there was another way a boy could train to be an actor. He could become a member of a "boys' company" or "children's company," a troupe made up exclusively of young boys and teens. Such companies were under the direction of adult masters, who supported and trained their youths and took the profits from their shows.

The Boys' Companies

Boys' companies generally performed in indoor private theaters, and often were closely associated with church choirs. One of the most prominent troupes, the Children of Paul's, was for many years associated with The Blackfriars, a private theater near St. Paul's Cathedral. Members of the boy troupes often were held in high regard for their singing abilities. Many were skilled musicians as well.

The plays written especially for the children's companies often took advantage of these musical gifts. These plays generally were shorter than average, giving the young actors time to perform an opening musical entertainment and play musical interludes between the acts.

Children's companies averaged ten or twelve players, more than was usual in an adult troupe. Perhaps this was because the managers of children's companies recognized that it was harder for young boys to memorize long sections of dialogue. Increasing the number of actors in a troupe would have decreased the need for doubling parts.

Noble Patrons

Whether a troupe was made up of adults or youths, all professional London troupes needed to find official patronage. Patrons were members of the nobility who lent prestige and political protection to the servants and employees in their care. The protection of a patron guarded a troupe from the possibility of facing criminal charges of vagrancy. Vagrancy—having no permanent home or job—was a serious crime, liable to result in severe punishments such as public whipping. Without patronage, actors were considered vagrants and "masterless men."

In 1572 a law had been passed that gave legal protection from this charge. Only those who were considered official servants of an "honourable personage," however, were exempt from vagrancy charges. If a London theater troupe became attached to such a patron, they were protected, and they had the considerable privilege of wearing the livery—the costume and colors—associated with that noble.

Troupes were named in honor of their patrons. From 1594 to 1596, for instance, Shakespeare belonged to a company sponsored by the first Lord Hunsdon, who held the important court position of lord chamberlain. When Lord Hunsdon died in 1596, his son, the second Lord Hunsdon, succeeded him as lord chamberlain. Under both men, the company was known as The Lord Chamberlain's Men. When James I succeeded Elizabeth in 1603, the troupe's patron changed. The new king singled

A portrait of King James I on horseback by the River Thames. Under King James, The Lord Chamberlain's Men enjoyed special favor, and the troupe was renamed The King's Men.

out the company for royal favor, and he renamed it The King's Men.

Sharing the Wealth

Some patrons essentially owned their troupes and the theaters in which the actors performed. In such cases the troupe paid rent to its patron and received salaries from him. In most cases, however, patrons did not directly support troupes financially. The actors had to be more or less self-sufficient.

Typically, troupes were cooperatively owned. Full members were usually the principal actors plus a manager and, in some cases, a writer. These full members were called "sharers." They held shares in the company, shared the costs of costumes and other expenditures, leased or owned their own theaters, and divided the profits.

Shares in a company could be very valuable. In 1595, the price of a share in either of the two leading companies, The Admiral's Men or The Lord Chamberlain's Men, was fifty pounds. To put this in perspective, the following year Shakespeare paid sixty pounds for a large house in his hometown of Stratford.

In addition to its principal members, the troupe hired nonsharing actors at fixed salaries to play small or secondary parts. Still more salaried workers took on a number of other tasks. They played music, served as prompters, created special effects, and did other odd jobs. A typical company had eight to twelve sharers, plus a fluctuating number of hired men and apprentices.

One nonsharing but important member of a troupe was the tire-man, who attired actors in their costumes and maintained the costumes when they were not in use. Another was the box-holder or gatherer, whose job was to collect admissions in a box as the audience came into a theater.

The Manager

The concept of a director, as a job separate from that of an actor or writer, had not yet developed in the Elizabethan era. Some scholars maintain that the job of director—instructing actors on where and when to move, how to speak their lines, and so on—was performed by actors and writers working together during rehearsal. Other theater historians disagree. Allardyce Nicoll, for one, feels that the job more or less took care of itself. He asserts that "because the Elizabethan playhouse had more or less established companies familiar with each other's skill, because this playhouse had no scenery or lighting, and because the age had a characteristic style of its own, the theatre needed no producer or director." [55]

In any case, another professional theatrical job did develop during the Elizabethan period: that of the manager. (The term "producer," which today generally describes a related function, was not used in Elizabethan times.) It was the manager's role to be responsible for the many practical and business aspects of putting on a play. This required the deft handling of many different tasks. Among them, according to theater historian Gerald Eades Bentley, were

authorizing the purchase of new costumes and costume materials; paying for new plays by free-lance dramatists; getting scripts approved by the Master of the Revels, paying him for licenses for the theater and for occasional privileges, like playing during parts of Lent; paying the company's regular contributions to the poor of the parish, assessing fines against sharers or hired men for infringement of company regulations; calling rehearsals; collecting fees for court and private

The purchase of costumes such as these burgher- and country-woman dresses was the responsibility of the theater manager.

performances; supervising the preparation and distribution of playbills and perhaps for paying the hired men. [56]

Henslowe

One of the top theatrical managers in London was Philip Henslowe. Henslowe managed, at various points in his career, The Rose, Hope, and Fortune theaters. These venues were either occupied by the company he managed, The Admiral's Men, or rented out to other companies.

Henslowe was a keen businessman, primarily involved in theater to make a profit. His usual arrangement was to take 50 percent of the gallery receipts from each performance in which he had a hand. In return, he took on all financial risks while mounting a play. He lent advances to his resident playwrights and actors, bought costumes and props, and assumed other expenses.

One reason Henslowe is prominent in Elizabethan theatrical history is that he kept an extensive journal that still exists and is the single best source of information modern historians have about the subject. This journal recounts his expenses and other information in detail. It reports, for instance, that Henslowe paid six pounds for Thomas Heywood's play *A Woman Killed*—a considerable sum in those days—and spent another seven on a velvet dress for the boy who played its leading role.

Henslowe was autocratic and overbearing toward his theaters, actors, and playwrights. He was known to charge high interest rates for loans to members of his troupe and to fine them harshly for such infractions as being tardy, absent, unruly, or drunk. Noting that The Lord Chamberlain's Men did not have such a domineering manager, historians Parrott and Ball comment, "It was fortunate for Shakespeare and his fellows that they were from the beginning independent of such a backer." [57]

The actors, managers, and others involved in London's theatrical world plied their trade to make money, of course, but also because they loved drama. They were joined in this love by the thousands of eager Londoners who formed their audience.

Chapter 7

The Elizabethan Audience

Elizabethan theater audiences came from all walks of life and so were a vivid cross-section of English society. In some ways, the people watching plays at The Globe or The Swan probably were as amusing and interesting as the "real" entertainment on stage. Thanks to the sweeping changes the Renaissance was providing, Elizabethans were keenly interested in learning as much as they could about the world around them. They made appreciative audiences for theater that challenged them as well as entertained them.

An Eager and Appreciative Audience

The world was changing quickly for the typical Elizabethan. Explorers returned from the Americas, Africa, and Asia with fantastic tales that fueled the populace's hunger for knowledge. Sweeping scientific, social, and religious changes were taking place all the time.

Meanwhile, after centuries of isolation, it was easier than ever for an Elizabethan to learn about the world outside his or her immediate experience. Although many Londoners still could not read, printing presses made it possible to create books cheaply and in quantity. Literacy was becoming more common, and the degree of education among all classes of people was higher than in previous times. Elizabethan playwrights and actors benefited from this increasingly educated audience, since they could refer to a broad scale of knowledge when creating their plays.

People went to the theater for the same reasons they now go to the theater or the movies—to relax, to witness spectacle and show, to appreciate artistry in acting and music, to escape for a while from their everyday lives. Attending a show was inexpensive entertainment, and everyone enjoyed it.

Nearly everyone did, at any rate. Some Londoners never went to the theater. Perhaps they objected on religious grounds, as did the Puritans, a group then growing in size and influence. Perhaps they could not afford even the modest admission price of a penny or two. Perhaps they could not afford to take an afternoon away from work. Or perhaps they simply did not like the theater.

In any event, London's population—about two hundred thousand—was more than enough to sustain a lively and exciting theater scene. Even if going to the theater was a foolish expenditure, many people did it anyway—even to the point of neglecting the most basic necessities. One observer of the time noted the "pinched, needy creatures, that live of alms [charitable donations], with scarce clothes for their backs or food for their bellies, make hard shift [try hard] that they will see a play, [and] let wife and children beg and languish in penury [poverty]."[58]

The majority of London's theaters lay on the southern bank of the River Thames, in the neighborhood known as Shoreditch. The Globe and The Bear Garden are visible in the foreground of this illustration.

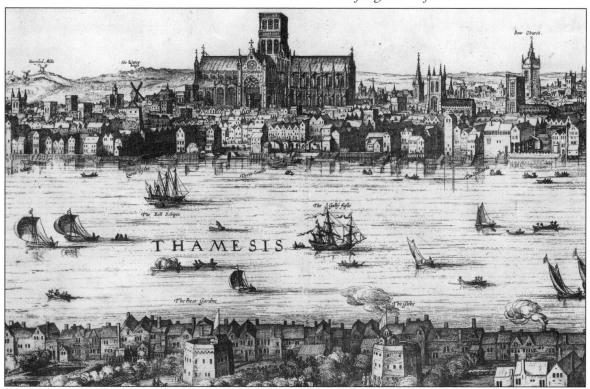

Getting There

If audiences found attending the theater an exciting event, simply getting there was half the fun. In Elizabethan England, venturing outside one's home neighborhood was unusual and thrilling for many people. A trip to a playhouse was a delightful and novel adventure.

Some of the major theaters in London were just north of the central city. Most, however, lay across the River Thames from the main City of London in Shoreditch, a neighborhood that had long been a center for low entertainment. Alehouses, prostitution, gambling, and animal-baiting were just a few of the thrills Shoreditch had to offer.

Nearly everyone came by foot. Shoreditch was a healthy walk from the center of town through narrow streets filled with colorful shops and sights, then across London Bridge. The bridge itself was a commercial center with bustling shops crowding both sides of a narrow walkway. This tradition of lining bridges with shops, a common practice in those days, still exists in a few European locations such as the famous Ponte Vecchio in Florence, Italy.

Those who preferred a less crowded route or enjoyed travel on the water could hire the services of a wherry-man to take them across the river. Wherry-men made their living ferrying passengers along the water in small boats, much as taxis transport people today.

The rise in the number of theaters in Shoreditch was a great boon to the wherry-men. In 1592 they had to petition Philip Henslowe to reopen a theater that had temporarily closed, informing him that the closure had hurt their business. They wrote: "wee your saide poore watermen have had muche helpe and reliefe for us oure poore wives and Children by meanes of the resorte of suche people as come unto the said playe howse." [59]

The Groundlings

Once they reached the general locale of the playhouse, audience members had to look to see if a flag was flying above it. If it was, then the play was set to be performed as scheduled. If not, the show was cancelled—perhaps because of bad weather.

Most theatergoers entered the building through a single main entrance on the opposite side of the theater from the stage's facade. Some privileged people, however, were admitted through a special entrance—the back door used by the actors.

Once inside, audience members paid a penny admission to the box-holder or gatherer. Those who could afford only this penny could stand during the show in the yard, the ground-level area around the stage. These people, appropriately, were called groundlings.

Groundlings were a rowdy bunch, quick to argue with each other and talk back to the actors—and, like most Elizabethans, never overly concerned with personal cleanliness. Thomas Dekker, a prominent playwright, once characterized them as "stinkards glued together in crowds with the steam of hot breath." [60] Another playwright, the cuttingly satirical Ben Jonson, called them a "rude

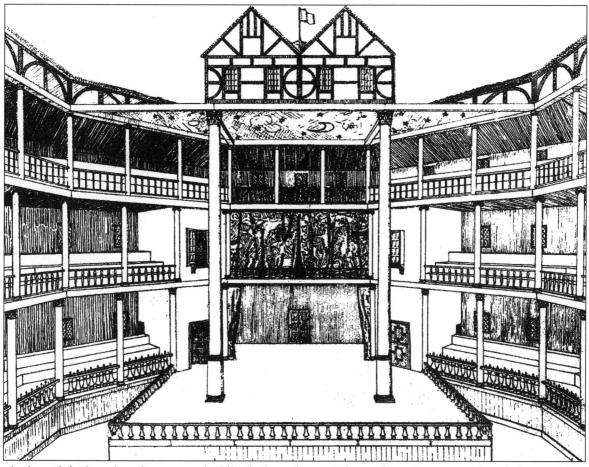

A view of the interior of an open-air Elizabethan theater. The yard or pit accommodated close to eight hundred spectators, while the gallery seated fifteen hundred.

barbarous crue, a people that haue [have] no brains." [61]

Jockeying for Space

If a little more money was paid to another gatherer—usually only an extra penny or two—an audience member could proceed further and find both a better vantage point and a bench on which to sit down. These were in the galleries that ringed the stage. Those who could afford still more—three pennies on top of what had already been spent—could sit in a private, closed-off room in the gallery. No matter where an audience member stood or sat, there were no reserved spaces. It was first come, first served, so everyone had to jostle everyone else for the best viewpoints.

Modern historians estimate that the yard of a typical open-air theater could hold about eight hundred people, while another fifteen hundred or so could fit in the galleries. The owners of the theaters naturally tried to cram in as many paying guests as possible. Even the galleries, therefore, were cramped and overcrowded. Those with seats could expect to have about two square feet for themselves. The groundlings, standing cheek-by-jowl in the yard, had even less room.

Bad Behavior

Audience members, as they found their seats or standing room and settled themselves in, were not particularly quiet or attentive to the needs of others. They laughed, flirted, and fidgeted. They ate apples and other snacks. They talked and gossiped and waited for the show.

Once the play got underway, things quieted down somewhat. If the play was boring or the actors inept, however, audiences did not hesitate to show their displeasure or simply talk among themselves and ignore the play.

Since theater stages of the day had no curtains separating the audiences from the actors, spectators were in especially intimate contact with performers. This left actors vulnerable if an audience felt like hurling abuse or rotten fruit, something they often did. On the other hand, audiences were quick to clap and cheer when they approved of the action onstage.

There is no evidence that anyone was ever ejected from an Elizabethan theater for rowdy behavior. It is doubtful whether a theater manager would have considered ejecting anyone for this reason; after all, rowdy patrons comprised the bulk of his paying audience.

Eat, Drink, and Make Money

Theater audiences loved to eat and drink, both before and during the show. To serve them, vendors sold food and drink such as apples, oranges, nuts, and tea before and during a performance. People sometimes brought their own snacks to plays, such as perfumed candy to sweeten the breath. However, food consumption was as closely controlled as it is in a modern sports stadium or theater. This was done strictly for financial reasons.

For instance, Philip Henslowe, always a hard-nosed businessman, arranged to create a monopoly on food sales in his theaters. In a contract with a partner, John Cholmley, Henslowe wrote: "He . . . will not permitte or suffer any personne or personnes other than the said John Cholmley . . . to vtter [either] sell or putt to sale in or aboute the said parcelle of grownde . . . any breade or drinke other than as shalbe solde to and the vse [use] and behoofe [behalf] of the saide John Cholmley." [62]

Smoking was also a common activity during theater performances. Tobacco was a recent introduction to England from the New World, and many Britons, including children, were avid smokers. It was commonly believed that tobacco was a medicine that would cure all manner of illness, including lung problems.

Ben Jonson made mention of the habit of smoking in the introduction to one of his plays, *Cynthia's Revels.* The play, which was debuted in 1600 by a "boy troupe," Queen Elizabeth's Children of the Chapel, is introduced by an actor who describes "an auditor" (listener) as saying:

Having paid my money at the door, with much ado, here I take my place and sit down: I have my three sorts of tobacco in my pocket and my light by me and thus I begin. (At this he breaks his tobacco.) By this light I wonder that any is so mad as to come to see these rascally tits' [birds'] plays—they do act like so many wrens or pismires—not the fifth part of a good face amongst them all—and their music is abominable. . . .

By this vapour, an t' were not for tobacco, I think the very stench of 'em would poison me, I should not dare to come in at their gates—A man were better visit fifteen jails or a dozen or two of hospitals than venture to come near them. [63]

"Anything but Aristocratic"

The theater in one respect was the most democratic institution in Elizabethan England. Class distinctions were extremely important in those times. The nobility, the merchant classes, the working classes, and the lower classes, generally speaking, did not mingle with one another. As theater audiences, however, the different classes did come together. They may have sat in different areas of the theater, but at least they were all in one place at one time. As theater historians Parrott and Ball note, "The Elizabethan theatre was anything but aristocratic." [64]

Many theater lovers were ordinary people: craftsmen, merchants, and other members of what we would now call the working or middle classes. Since the cheapest admission was only a penny, it was an affordable entertainment that even the poorest usually could afford.

Mixing freely with these ordinary people were others who came from different social classes and occupations. A typical audience might include a lively mix of noblemen and noblewomen, travelers from other countries, soldiers on leave, wealthy merchants, students, beggars, thieves, prostitutes, and more. Writer C. Walter Hodges notes wryly that "beggars, bullies, pickpockets and drunkards were as fond of entertainment as ladies and gentlemen were." [65]

The Elizabethan theater was, perhaps, the only venue where this aristocratic lady (left) would have come together with this country woman (right).

Gallants

On the other hand, the differences between public and private theaters did create a division between the types of audience that frequented those theaters. The higher price and plusher atmosphere of the private the-aters naturally attracted a more polished and aristocratic audience.

The differences in audiences and venues found in public and private theaters no doubt affected the ways in which actors performed. The intimate surroundings and select audi-

A troupe of itinerant players stages a private performance for wealthy theater patrons.

ence of a private theater were quite different from that of the more boisterous open-air public theaters. Historian James Roose-Evans notes, "A standing audience is more volatile than a seated one, and it is one thing to declaim to an audience of two thousand people eating fruit, smoking tobacco, gossiping, and quite another to play before an intimate, sophisticated company of some two hundred educated men." [66]

The audiences in private theaters were not always polite, however. Groups of dandified young men were notorious for disrupting performances, especially in the smaller and more exclusive private theaters. These young men were called "gallants." They were wealthy members of the aristocracy, and as such they comprised a dominant force in London high society.

For the hefty sum of sixpence (six pennies) each, these upper-crust dandies could purchase seats right on the stage of the theater. They then hired the apprentices attached to the theater's troupe of players to scurry off and find whatever they needed— a stool on which to sit, perhaps, or a tobacco pipe.

The gallants were not really there to watch the play, however, and rarely paid attention. They were strictly there to be seen. They gambled with cards and dice, gossiped among themselves, and sat posing so that their expensive clothes could be displayed to best advantage. The gallants undoubtedly were terrible nuisances to both the players and the rest of the audience, but because they could pay well they were tolerated.

Women and Children

In the Elizabethan era women were generally considered weaker and less intelligent than men. According to the social customs of the day, they were fit to be little more than housewives sheltered from the rougher edges of life. Nonetheless, Elizabethan women were allowed to attend public theaters as long as they were properly chaperoned.

Surprisingly, from what scholars and historians can discern, it appears that there was little ill feeling among the general population toward women attending plays. This was probably especially true among the working class, where the standards of "proper" morality were somewhat more relaxed than in the upper reaches of society.

Children could attend the theater as well, although they probably did not come in large numbers. In Elizabethan time children were generally allowed less freedom and fewer free-time luxuries, such as attending a form of entertainment, than they are today. Instead, they were expected to work all day or to attend school and then perform their chores around the home. Cost was undoubtedly also a factor. A poor man who could barely afford a penny admission for himself would think twice about bringing along a family that might include eight or ten children.

Dressing Up

Unlike the gallants, most people did not dress extravagantly when they attended the theater. The poorer members of the audience wore what they wore every day:

homemade dresses, smocks, breeches, cloaks, and caps. Their wealthier counterparts could afford to dress up for the theater in more elegant clothing, even if it was not as fancy or luxurious as that of the gallants.

For men, this style of clothing typically meant thick woolen capes, embroidered jackets, delicately painted gloves, and starched, pleated collars called ruffs. Women wore even more elaborate costumes than their male counterparts. These included petticoats, tight corsets, heavy skirts, and heavily embroidered dresses with detachable sleeves and enormous ruffs.

Although it was not the fashion for men at the time to wear wigs, many women did. These wigs were typically made of human hair, although materials such as silk or gold wire were sometimes also used. In part, the custom of wearing wigs was simply to follow the fashion of Queen Elizabeth. Bess was famously a redhead, but she wore a wig to cover her thinning hair in her later years.

Pickpockets and Cutpurses

Whether elegantly dressed or simply clothed, theatergoers had to be careful of thieves at all times. The criminal class was one element of society that was sure to be found in any large gathering in Elizabethan London—including the theater.

Two of the most common kinds of thieves to specialize in working crowds were the aptly named pickpocket and cutpurse. Pickpockets used their nimble hands and fingers to reach into the pockets of unsuspecting theatergoers and lift out a purse or wallet. Cutpurses used somewhat cruder methods; with small, sharp knives, they sliced through the leather holding a purse to its owner's belt and made off with it.

Playgoers provided these thieves with plenty of other valuable items to steal besides purses and wallets. Wealthy patrons, both men and women, loved to attend the theater wearing fancy jewelry such as necklaces, earrings, and pins. They also adorned their clothes with valuable buttons made of ivory or gold.

Such baubles were ripe pickings, and no one was immune. Even Queen Elizabeth, who was constantly surrounded by royal guards, was known to occasionally lose jewels or buttons from her dresses. It is likely that these were snipped off in secret by those sitting next to the queen when she attended official banquets or the pageants and entertainments she loved. While the jewels were undoubtedly taken as souvenirs, not as something to be sold again, this gives some indication of how easy it was to steal from even a closely guarded royal personage.

Royal Audiences

At the top of the scale of audiences, as far as England's class structure was concerned, were the queen herself and the noblemen and noblewomen who comprised the court surrounding her. London's top acting troupes were often called upon to perform in the houses of these members of nobility, especially in the case of patrons and the

A troupe of actors performs for Queen Elizabeth. Such performances were given only by royal invitation, and were always in the queen's honor.

troupes to whom the nobles lent their name. If a troupe of players was held in special favor, it would also be invited to appear at the royal court on a regular basis for command performances. The Admiral's Men and The Lord Chamberlain's Men were the two troupes most often invited to perform at court in this manner.

Queen Elizabeth was an enthusiastic audience for these performances held in her honor. She knew a great deal about the theater arts and had high standards. The queen was quick to show her appreciation of a particular performance—and quick to voice her disapproval. She was known to call out to actors or to move her chair nearer if she could not hear the play properly.

Elizabeth and her courtiers made excellent audiences. They were accustomed to a lavish way of life that catered to their every whim, and so they accepted entertainment performed by others as a God-given right—even if those others were considered somewhat disreputable actors.

Theater as Politics

To these nobles, such entertainment was something to be thoroughly enjoyed, and so they were tolerant of the eccentricities of actors—more tolerant, perhaps, than average public audiences, and certainly more so than those religious conservatives who disliked the theater. The queen and her courtiers thus did all they could to patronize and protect the more reputable companies of players.

Elizabeth had other reasons for fostering and encouraging the theater troupes that fell under the wings of her courtiers. She certainly enjoyed theater simply as theater. Asking a particular troupe to appear at court was, however, more than simple enjoyment of the theater for the queen. It was also a means of political persuasion.

Elizabeth was constantly preoccupied with maintaining a balance of power and dependence among the many aristocrats who flocked around her. She was a very shrewd judge of these courtiers, and she was always looking for ways to put them in good or bad favor, depending on her ulterior motive.

She understood that favoring a specific troupe put that troupe's patron in a good light. If she wanted to flatter a courtier she would compliment him by asking his troupe to appear before her. Drama historian Peter Thomson points out, "The royal command to perform at court may have flattered the players, but it should not be forgotten that it flattered their patrons too."[67]

Elizabeth's control over the theater was strong as long as she remained a strong monarch. Toward the end of her reign, however, she was beginning to lose some of her power. The extraordinary sense of unity and security England felt during most of her reign was beginning to erode—and along with it the Elizabethan era's theatrical world began to change.

The Decline of the Elizabethan Theater

In many ways, London's public and private theaters flourished in the final years of Elizabeth's reign. The queen continued to enjoy command performances at court as well. She enjoyed them so much, in fact, that in 1601 she ordered the construction of the first permanent stage in a royal building, in the Banqueting Hall of the Palace of Whitehall.

However, the life of the queen—an extraordinarily long one by the standards of the day—was growing short. On February 2, 1603, The Lord Chamberlain's Men received what would be their final summons to perform before her. The Admiral's Men performed for her on March 6 in what also proved to be a last performance. Less than three weeks later, at age seventy, the queen was dead.

Her cousin, James VI of Scotland, succeeded her. As king of England, he was renamed James I. The mood of the nation, and the nature of the court, changed dramatically as the Elizabethan regime made a transition to the new era, which was called Jacobean in James's honor. The world of the theater changed as well.

A Shift in Mood
The first decades of Elizabeth's long reign had been a period of optimism, strength, and forward movement for England. A key event had been the English navy's massive, unexpected victory in 1588 over its longtime enemy, Spain.

After this and other triumphs, Elizabeth brought her country together as it had never

The Spanish and English navies meet in a decisive battle in 1588. The English victory over the Spanish Armada ushered in a period of great prosperity for England.

been before. Under her rule England felt more secure, experienced tremendous feelings of patriotism, and felt a newfound sense of national unity. During the first quarter-century or so of her reign, Good Queen Bess had turned her country around. Once England had been a small and relatively isolated island nation, torn apart by religious battles. Under her, it had become a strong empire that, while still experiencing religious trouble, was more closely united than ever before.

Playwrights had been quick to mirror this sense of optimism, security, and patriotism in their work. Summing up this feeling was a character in Shakespeare's *Richard II* who delivers an impassioned tribute to England. He refers to the nation as "this scepter'd isle. . . . This fortress built by Nature for herself/Against infection and the hand of war." He then compares the sea around the island nation to "a moat defensive to a house/Against the envy of less happier lands." Moreover, he refers to the English people as "this happy breed of men, this little world."[68]

However, the national mood of optimism began to change in the latter part of the century. Elizabeth's reign began to suffer a succession of problems. One of these was a worsening economy that forced Elizabeth to raise taxes sharply and eroded her popularity. Another was a long battle, expensive both in lives and money, to suppress rebellion in Ireland.

Still another was Elizabeth's controversial action concerning her devoutly Catholic cousin, Mary, Queen of Scots. (This ruler should not be confused with Elizabeth's half-sister, also Mary.) English Catholics hoped to replace Protestant Elizabeth with the Catholic Mary, so Elizabeth, fearing that her cousin was a threat, ordered Mary's execution. The move outraged many and further chipped away at Elizabeth's popularity. By the end of the 1500s England was in stormy shape. Writer Christine Eccles notes that "the economy was nearly bankrupt, plague was endemic, the Queen was ageing and the national mood had swung." [69]

Changes in Royal Style

James's ascension to the throne did nothing to help the feelings of unease. Elizabeth had been a symbol of stability and strength, but James was unable to sustain the support she had enjoyed. The new king's attitude made him unpopular with nearly everyone; commoners and nobility alike found him arrogant, overbearing, and inept.

The two monarchs were very different in their personal styles. Elizabeth had always been financially frugal; James was reckless and extravagant in his spending, both for himself and for the nation. Elizabeth was famously known as "the virgin Queen," making herself into a symbol of purity and correct behavior. James, however, was open about his promiscuity and bisexuality. Furthermore, Elizabeth had granted royal

honors sparingly, but James helped subsidize his lavish spending by selling honors such as knighthoods to anyone with the cash.

James did do some lasting good. For one thing, he made peace with England's

Mary, Queen of Scots, readies herself for death. The Protestant Queen Elizabeth identified her Catholic cousin, Mary, as a threat to her authority, and ordered her execution.

old enemy, Spain. He also arranged for an important new translation of the Bible—the famous King James Version. Nonetheless, he was an inadequate leader. Preoccupied with the intrigues of his court, he ignored growing unrest and dissatisfaction in his country—a discontent that eventually led to civil war.

Changes in the Theater

James's ascension to king had a major effect on London theater. The new king enjoyed and actively supported drama, as had Elizabeth, but in very different ways. Though in many regards things continued as before, the difference was clear. Theater historians Parrott and Ball note, "The influence of the [new] Court upon late Elizabethan drama is unmistakeable." [70]

Part of the change that took place in the London theaters had nothing to do with James's rule, but was a coincidence of fate. An especially severe outbreak of the plague took place in 1603, the same year James became king. The disease claimed some thirty thousand lives in London alone that year, and because of it the theaters were closed for almost a year.

The closure of the theaters naturally made life uncertain for everyone who was connected with them. Actors, writers, and anyone else who worked in the playhouses had to scramble for alternate ways of making a living. Shakespeare, for one, devoted this period to writing much of his immortal poetry.

Actors were still able to work as actors despite the shuttering of the theaters, although to a lesser degree. James loved the theater and encouraged his Master of the Revels to arrange many royal performances. Some players even were able to perform at the royal court, and at the homes of the nobility, more often than they had previously.

One measure of this is the number of plays mounted at court during the Christmas season. For the five years before Elizabeth's death, an average of six plays had been performed expressly for her during this season. In just the first season of James's reign, however, there were sixteen such plays.

The King's Men

There were many demonstrations of change in the theater world as the Elizabethan age became the Jacobean age. One reflected both James's love of theater and his desire to control the best of it.

Almost immediately after becoming king, he required that the leading companies come under his direct control. This meant that they were obliged to serve under royal patronage rather than merely noble patronage. In essence, James stole his favorite players away from his courtiers and gave them to himself or his family.

In this way, Worcester's Men, one of the top troupes, became Queen Anne's Men in honor of James's wife. The Admiral's Men came under the patronage of the heir to the throne, Prince Henry. Meanwhile, The Lord Chamberlain's Men, the troupe that Shakespeare was associated with, came under the direct patronage of James himself and was renamed The King's Men.

A scene from a modern production of the Jacobean comedy, A Chaste Maid in Cheapside. *English theater underwent many changes under the reign of King James I.*

In return for their prestigious royal licenses all of these actors were obliged to entertain at court on a regular basis. Once the theaters reopened they also could resume their public performances. When they began these public shows again, The King's Men continued to perform for a few seasons at The Globe.

Less Public, More Private

James's love and fostering of theater affected the London scene in many ways. Perhaps the major change was a marked difference in how and where acting troupes performed. James's courtiers copied his attention to the theater. They began to support actors, and theater in general, far more than before. This meant both increased patronage and increased attendance at the theater. In turn, this support changed the ways in which theater was written and performed, as troupes tried to please these newly attentive patrons.

One result of this was a new trend away from the open-air theaters in favor of indoor, private theaters. These more refined settings were sheltered from the elements, equipped with seats, lit with candles for evening performances, and even heated. This made them far better suited to the tastes of a new brand of audience.

The King's Men spearheaded this movement. When the theaters reopened after the plague closings, the troupe played at The Globe for only a few shortened summer seasons. In 1608 the players took a long-term lease on a private theater, The Blackfriars.

Other troupes followed this lead and began favoring indoor theaters as well. Established public theaters such as The Globe and The Fortune still continued their activities to a degree. However, by far the bulk of the new plays was now produced at private theaters. Furthermore, new theaters

A view of The Fortune theater in London. The Fortune continued to prosper under James I, despite the fact that most new plays were produced in private theaters.

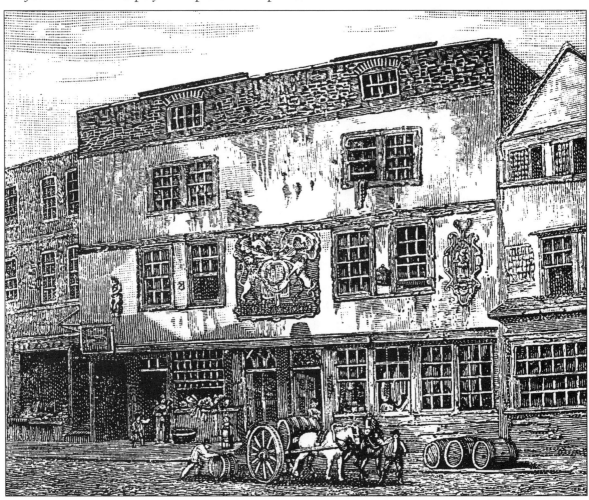

that were built in London from this time on were mostly indoor houses. The most prominent of these was The Cockpit, later known as The Phoenix.

New Players, New Styles

Another change in theatrical fashion during this period was the demise of troupes made up entirely of boy players. One reason for this was a series of satires produced by a prominent boys' troupe, The Children of the Queen's Revels. These satires were scandalously daring, touching closely upon the personal and political failings of King James. Among these plays were *Eastward Ho,* written by Ben Jonson, John Marston, and George Chapman, and *The Isle of Gulls* by John Day.

A furious James revoked the royal patronage of The Children of the Queen's Revels, and in 1606 the troupe was forced to dissolve. Shortly after, other prominent boys' troupes began to cease operation as well. Many of the young men who had been in these companies found work with adult troupes, but the era of the boy troupes was essentially over.

Another change in the theater was the emergence of several new styles of dramatic writing. This came about largely as a natural result of actors playing before more sophisticated and educated audiences. The new audience was increasingly preoccupied with the intrigues of life at court and the etiquette of life among the aristocracy.

One new style that took advantage of these interests was an exceptionally light and witty brand of comedy. Later in the

seventeenth century this style would come to be called the comedy of manners. This sophisticated comic style shed a kindly light on the lives and loves of the upper crust of society—the lords and ladies, the well-to-do and cultured citizens. In contrast, its biting satire was often directed against those lower on the social scale: vulgar shopkeepers and merchants or simple country folk.

Another new style, the tragicomedy, also came into favor during this period. As the name implies, tragicomedies mixed elements of tragedy and comedy into a single dramatic form—but they always ended happily.

Changing with the Times

As tastes changed, professional writers followed the wishes of their new patrons and audiences, generally writing what they knew would be popular. They succeeded if they were able to adapt their writing styles to the tastes of these audiences.

Shakespeare was one writer who was able to move with the times. As a member of The King's Men, he naturally had to write plays that would please the new king. An example of these is his great tragedy *Macbeth,* which has a Scottish setting reflecting James's background.

Taken as a whole, Shakespeare's output over his long career reflected changes in national temperament. His early plays, written during the times of optimism, generally reflected the positive attitude in England. Even the histories and the tragedy *Romeo and Juliet* have many moments that are exuberant and sunny. After 1600, however, Shakespeare concentrated on tragedies. In

A scene from a modern production of Shakespeare's Measure for Measure, *a comedy that reflects much of the turbulence of the Jacobean era.*

his later years these became increasingly confused, gloomy, and even bitter. Even his comedies from this period, such as *Measure for Measure* and *All's Well That Ends Well,* have a dark quality.

Old Writers, New Era

As the Jacobean era moved on, the older generation of writers, including Shakespeare, moved aside to make room for younger playwrights. Shakespeare was writing less and less, slowing down his remarkable output.

He split his last years between London and Stratford, his hometown, in semiretirement. He died in 1616 and was buried in Stratford.

Ben Jonson, meanwhile, emerged as the premiere playwright of his generation who was intimately involved in writing for the royal court. He wrote few plays for the popular stage later in his career. He specialized instead in creating masques for James's court. In 1616 he received a handsome pension from the king and essentially became the nation's poet laureate.

Jonson continued to work even after suffering a stroke, a series of failures on the popular stage, and bitter quarrels with former associates. He died in 1637 and was buried in Westminster Abbey under a plain slab. The memorial was later carved with the inscription, "O Rare Ben Jonson!"

In the opinion of many scholars, Jonson was more influential and important during his life than Shakespeare. Parrott and Ball assert, "Today the name of Shakespeare seems to stand as the supreme representative of drama in the Elizabethan era. It was not so in his own day." [71]

Other Writers

A number of writers stepped in to take the places of scribes such as Shakespeare and Jonson. One prominent playwright was John Webster, whose *The Duchess of Malfi* is generally regarded as a masterpiece of tragedy. The prolific Francis Beaumont was a prominent Jacobean satirist. In plays such as *The Knight of the Burning Pestle,* Beaumont

A scene from a modern production of John Webster's The Duchess of Malfi. *Webster was one of several playwrights who rose to prominence as Shakespeare's career was coming to an end.*

ridiculed earlier dramas and romances about elegant heroes; at the same time, he also satirized the newly rich merchant class.

Still another prominent writer of the period was John Fletcher, whose hallmarks were an easy style and great sophistication. Fletcher followed in Shakespeare's footsteps when he became ordinary poet for The King's Men after Shakespeare's retirement. For many years, Fletcher's plays were as highly praised as Shakespeare's and Jonson's.

Fletcher had a gift for creating strong action and emotional scenes, and is best remembered for his tragicomedies. A representative example is *A Wife for a Month,* in which a tyrant tries to seduce a chaste woman. When she resists him, he arranges for her to marry her true love—but only for a month, after which he dies and she must remarry. Despite the strangeness of this situation, the play, as befit the fashion, ends happily.

Fletcher and Beaumont collaborated often, creating together a popular series of romances and tragicomedies. Among their joint successes were *Philaster, The Maid's Tragedy,* and *A King and No King.* There is some evidence that Fletcher and Beaumont may also have worked with Shakespeare on his last plays, *Henry VIII* and *The Two Noble Kinsmen.*

Three other prominent playwrights from this period were Thomas Middleton, Cyril Tourneur, and Philip Massinger. Massinger wrote almost forty plays, often for The King's Men, and frequently collaborated with others. He is best known for his comedy *A New Way to Pay Old Debts.* Its chief character, the villain Sir Giles Overreach, was so popular a figure that during the seventeenth century the play was performed more often than any other non-Shakespearean play.

Jacobean Masques

Progressively, the influence of the royal court's attention to theater was seen in a revived interest in masques. Under James's influence, masques became not only more frequent but also increasingly elaborate.

James and his queen both loved these intricate, expensive affairs. James appreciated the references to classical stories and learning, while his wife simply loved to dress up and dance. Unlike Elizabeth, both were willing to spend lavishly to have masques created for them. For one particularly openhanded affair, they spent the truly extravagant sum of three thousand pounds.

As a result of James's attention, masques developed into extremely intricate affairs. They featured music by the best composers, complicated scenery (both stationary and movable), and texts by top poets and playwrights.

Among the twenty-odd masques Jonson wrote for James were *The Masque of Blacknesse, The Masque of Owles,* and *The Masque of Beauty.* These pageants put the writer's scholarship, wit, versatility, and gift for lyric poetry to good use, especially his frequent collaborations with the innovative set designer Inigo Jones.

One of Jonson's contributions to the masque form was the development of a prologue, called the antemasque. The antemasque featured grotesque or comic ele-

A group of costumed revelers prepares for a masque. The colorful spectacle and vibrant action of the masque made it one of the most popular theatrical genres of the Jacobean era.

ments that contrasted with the elegance of the main part of the masque. Jonson was able to insert cuttingly satirical pieces into these prologues, so cleverly woven into the main fabric of the entertainment that they went almost unnoticed by their audiences.

In time, however, Jonson had to retire from the scene. He quarreled with Jones, their partnership dissolved, and after Jonson suffered his stroke he was not able to work much. Many scholars feel that once Jonson faded from prominence, the art of the masque lost its high literary value. Masques became simply vehicles for spectacle with vulgar scenery and costumes overshadowing any true dramatic content.

By Popular Demand

The influence of the masque was long lasting, however. For one thing, it was a direct influence on grand opera, a style of musical entertainment that was starting to develop, primarily in Italy, during this period.

The high spectacle associated with masques also made itself felt in regular playwriting and acting. Reports of the lavish one-time-only masques performed before royalty spread among those who had no access to court and thus could not see them. Theatergoers were so eager to witness these spectacles that they began to mob what were meant to be private performances. The performance of Beaumont's *Masque of Gray's*

Inn and the Inner Temple, for example, had to be postponed because an intruding crowd created such a disturbance that the show could not go on.

Playwrights began introducing elements of the masque into their work for public theaters. One of these elements was a style of comic dance, used as an interlude in the action of the play. The Morris dance in Fletcher and Shakespeare's *The Two Noble Kinsmen* was borrowed directly from a masque written by Beaumont. Some plays of the era contained masques within them, such as the masque that serves as an interlude in John Marston's *Antonio's Revenge.*

Gradually, elements of stagecraft originally used strictly for masques, such as elaborate scenery, were introduced to the public theater as well. Such components of stagecraft in time became standard elements of the public theater.

An important example of this was William Davenant's *The Siege of Rhodes* (full title: *The Siege of Rhodes Made a Representation by the Art of Prospective in Scenes, And the story Sung in Recitative Musick*). Produced in 1656, *The Siege of Rhodes* is generally considered the first publicly performed opera in English. It calls for five full changes of painted scenery. It is also notable for introducing a daring new element to the English stage: the female performer.

The Closing of the Theaters

The theater remained a popular pastime until 1642, when the Puritans came to power in England. This group of religious conservatives condemned the theater for several reasons. They believed, first and foremost, that plays were wicked because they had nothing to do with God. They also were upset at the use of boys on stage in women's roles, even if this practice was dwindling. Further, the Puritans saw a connection between the theater and the plague. "The cause of plagues is sin, if you look to it well," warned one Puritan leader, "and the cause of sin are plays; therefore the cause of plagues are plays." [72]

Once in power, the Puritans ordered all theaters closed. The Globe, where many of Shakespeare's plays had debuted, was torn down to make way for public housing. The closure order remained in effect until 1656, shortly before the reign of King Charles II ushered in a new period in English history, the Restoration. This shuttering of the theaters marked the definitive end for a period many theater historians consider the richest and most varied time in the history of English drama—the Elizabethan era.

Notes

Chapter 1: A Golden Age of Theater

1. Thomas Marc Parrott and Robert Hamilton Ball, *A Short View of Elizabethan Drama.* New York: Charles Scribner's Sons, 1958, pp. 290–94.
2. R.C. Bald, ed., *Six Elizabethan Plays.* Boston: Houghton Mifflin, 1963, p. vii.
3. Quoted in Ian W. Archer, "Shakespeare's London," in David Scott Kastan, ed., *A Companion to Shakespeare.* Malden, MA: Blackwell, 1999, p. 45.
4. Simon Trussler, *The Cambridge Illustrated History of English Theatre.* Cambridge, UK: Cambridge University Press, 1994, p. 101.
5. Quoted in Editors of Horizon Magazine, *Shakespeare's England.* New York: Harper & Row, 1964, p. 34.

Chapter 2: The Origins of the Elizabethan Theater

6. J.L. Styan, *The English Stage: A History of Drama and Performance.* Cambridge, UK: Cambridge University Press, 1996, p. 8.
7. David Klein, *Milestones to Shakespeare.* New York: Twayne, 1970, p. 2.
8. Styan, *The English Stage*, p. 17.
9. Klein, *Milestones to Shakespeare*, p. 5.
10. Styan, *The English Stage*, p. 3.
11. Parrott and Ball, *A Short View of Elizabethan Drama*, p. 14.
12. Styan, *The English Stage*, p. 56.
13. Quoted in Styan, *The English Stage*, p. 75.

Chapter 3: The London Theaters

14. Trussler, *The Cambridge Illustrated History of English Theatre*, p. 71.
15. Quoted in Christine Eccles, *The Rose Theatre.* New York: Routledge/Theatre Arts Books, 1990, p. 1.
16. Quoted in Editors of Horizon Magazine, *Shakespeare's England*, p. 91.
17. James Roose-Evans, *London Theatre: From the Globe to the National.* Oxford, UK: Phaidon, 1977, p. 19.
18. Styan, *The English Stage*, p. 92.
19. Eccles, *The Rose Theatre*, p. 6.
20. Eccles, *The Rose Theatre*, p. 85.
21. Quoted in Roose-Evans, *London Theatre*, p. 17.
22. Styan, *The English Stage*, p. 99.

Chapter 4: Between Heaven and Hell: Stagecraft

23. Alan C. Dessen, *Elizabethan Drama and the Viewer's Eye*. Chapel Hill:

University of North Carolina Press, 1977, p. 14.

24. Quoted in Dessen, *Elizabethan Drama and the Viewer's Eye*, p. 13.

25. Quoted in Dessen, *Elizabethan Drama and the Viewer's Eye*, p. 72.

26. Roose-Evans, *London Theatre*, p. 17.

27. Peter Thomson, *Shakespeare's Professional Career*. Cambridge, UK: Cambridge University Press, 1992, p. 93.

28. Thomson, *Shakespeare's Professional Career*, p. 94.

29. Ivor Brown, *How Shakespeare Spent the Day*. New York: Hill & Wang, 1963, p. 104.

30. Quoted in Dessen, *Elizabethan Drama and the Viewer's Eye*, p. 14.

31. Eccles, *The Rose Theatre*, p. 4.

Chapter 5: Ordinary Poets: Elizabethan Playwrights

32. Scott McMillin, "Professional Playwrighting," in Kastan, *A Companion to Shakespeare*, p. 230.

33. Eccles, *The Rose Theatre*, p. 63.

34. Quoted in Thomson, *Shakespeare's Professional Career*, p. 83.

35. Thomas Whitfield Baldwin, *The Organization and Personnel of the Shakespearean Company*. New York: Russell and Russell, 1927, p. 284.

36. McMillin, "Professional Playwrighting," p. 227.

37. Quoted in Bald, *Six Elizabethan Plays*, pp. 69–70.

38. Parrott and Ball, *A Short View of Elizabethan Drama*, p. 95.

39. William Shakespeare, *The Complete Works of William Shakespeare*. New York: Garden City, 1936, p. 749.

40. Shakespeare, *The Complete Works of William Shakespeare*, p. 699.

41. Parrott and Ball, *A Short View of Elizabethan Drama*, p. 109.

42. Parrott and Ball, *A Short View of Elizabethan Drama*, p. 91.

43. Quoted in Bald, *Six Elizabethan Plays*, pp. xi–xii.

44. Quoted in Thomson, *Shakespeare's Professional Career*, p. 131.

Chapter 6: Treading the Boards: Actors

45. Thomson, *Shakespeare's Professional Career*, p. 87.

46. Quoted in Eccles, *The Rose Theatre*, p. 56.

47. Thomson, *Shakespeare's Professional Career*, p. 81.

48. McMillin, "Professional Playwrighting," p. 230.

49. McMillin, "Professional Playwrighting," p. 231.

50. W. Robertson Davies, *Shakespeare's Boy Actors*. New York: Russell and Russell, 1964, p. 30.

51. Thomson, *Shakespeare's Professional Career*, p. 108.

52. Davies, *Shakespeare's Boy Actors*, p. 31.

53. Quoted in Thomson, *Shakespeare's Professional Career*, p. 52.

54. Davies, *Shakespeare's Boy Actors*, p. 3.
55. Quoted in Brown, *How Shakespeare Spent the Day*, p. 88.
56. Gerald Eades Bentley, *The Profession of Player in Shakespeare's Time*. Princeton, NJ: Princeton University Press, 1984, p. 148.
57. Parrott and Ball, *A Short View of Elizabethan Drama*, p. 95.

Chapter 7: The Elizabethan Audience

58. Quoted in Brown, *How Shakespeare Spent the Day*, p. 29.
59. Quoted in Thomson, *Shakespeare's Professional Career*, p. 70.
60. Quoted in Roose-Evans, *London Theatre*, p. 20.
61. Quoted in Eccles, *The Rose Theatre*, p. 30.
62. Quoted in Eccles, *The Rose Theatre*, p. iii.

63. Quoted in Brown, *How Shakespeare Spent the Day*, p. 80.
64. Parrott and Ball, *A Short View of Elizabethan Drama*, p. 48.
65. C. Walter Hodges, *Shakespeare's Theatre*. New York: Coward-McCann, 1964, p. 46.
66. Roose-Evans, *London Theatre*, p. 23.
67. Thomson, *Shakespeare's Professional Career*, p. 30.

Chapter 8: The Decline of the Elizabethan Theater

68. Shakespeare, *The Complete Works of William Shakespeare*, p. 360.
69. Eccles, *The Rose Theatre*, pp. 3–4.
70. Parrott and Ball, *A Short View of Elizabethan Drama*, p. 183.
71. Parrott and Ball, *A Short View of Elizabethan Drama*, p. 127.
72. Quoted in Editors of Horizon Magazine, *Shakespeare's England*, p. 57.

For Further Reading

John Russell Brown, *Shakespeare and His Theatre.* New York: Lothrop, Lee & Shepard, 1982. A look at how The Globe appeared and operated, written by a Shakespearean scholar, with charming illustrations by David Gentleman.

Marshall Cavendish, *Exploring the Past: Shakespeare's England.* Freeport, NY: Marshall Cavendish, 1989. A heavily illustrated book focusing on Shakespeare, Elizabeth I, and her father, Henry VIII.

Editors of Horizon Magazine, *Shakespeare's England.* New York: Harper & Row, 1964. A nicely illustrated and clearly written overview.

C. Walter Hodges, *Shakespeare's Theatre.* New York: Coward-McCann, 1964. An entertaining book with attractive illustrations by the author.

Works Consulted

R.C. Bald, ed., *Six Elizabethan Plays.* Boston: Houghton Mifflin, 1963. A reprint of six plays representing different aspects of Elizabethan theater, with a useful introduction.

Thomas Whitfield Baldwin, *The Organization and Personnel of the Shakespearean Company.* New York: Russell and Russell, 1927. A classic and thorough work of scholarship.

Gerald Eades Bentley, *The Profession of Player in Shakespeare's Time.* Princeton, NJ: Princeton University Press, 1984. A scholarly study by a professor of English.

Ivor Brown, *How Shakespeare Spent the Day.* New York: Hill & Wang, 1963. A clearly written and lively account of daily life in the Elizabethan theater.

W. Robertson Davies, *Shakespeare's Boy Actors.* New York: Russell and Russell, 1964. A lively history by a distinguished Canadian author and theater critic.

Alan C. Dessen, *Elizabethan Drama and the Viewer's Eye.* Chapel Hill: University of North Carolina Press, 1977. This volume by a scholar of the subject is primarily for actors and directors.

Christine Eccles, *The Rose Theatre.* New York: Routledge/Theatre Arts Books, 1990. An account of the discovery in 1989 and subsequent restoration of the remains of an important Elizabethan theater.

David Scott Kastan, ed., *A Companion to Shakespeare.* Malden, MA: Blackwell, 1999. A valuable compendium of short essays.

David Klein, *Milestones to Shakespeare.* New York: Twayne, 1970. A scholarly work with extensive quotations from pre-Shakespearean English drama.

Thomas Marc Parrott and Robert Hamilton Ball, *A Short View of Elizabethan Drama.* New York: Charles Scribner's Sons, 1958. A classic work by two experts.

James Roose-Evans, *London Theatre: From the Globe to the National.* Oxford, UK: Phaidon, 1977. This lively history includes a chapter on the Elizabethan and Jacobean eras.

William Shakespeare, *The Complete Works of William Shakespeare.* New York: Garden City, 1936. One of many editions of the works of the Bard of Avon.

J.L. Styan, *The English Stage: A History of Drama and Performance.* Cambridge, UK: Cambridge University Press, 1996. Although written by a scholar, this is a lucid text for the lay reader.

Peter Thomson, *Shakespeare's Professional Career*. Cambridge, UK: Cambridge University Press, 1992. A well-illustrated book that focuses on how Shakespeare adapted himself to the fashions and conventions of his time.

Simon Trussler, *The Cambridge Illustrated History of English Theatre*. Cambridge, UK: Cambridge University Press, 1994. This beautifully illustrated book is an ample source of information.

John Dover Wilson, *Life in Shakespeare's England: A Book of Elizabethan Prose*. Cambridge, UK: Cambridge University Press, 1913. Focuses on writings from the Elizabethan period.

Index

Picture Credits

About the Author

Adam Woog has written more than thirty books for adults, young adults, and children. Among his books for Lucent are volumes on Harry Houdini, Roosevelt and the New Deal, and the history of rock and roll. He lives with his wife and daughter in his hometown of Seattle, Washington.